When These Things Begin

Studies in Violence, Mimesis, and Culture

When These Things Begin

René Girard

Conversations with Michel Treguer

Translated by Trevor Cribben Merrill

Michigan State University Press · *East Lansing*

⊛ The paper used in this publication meets the minimum requirements of ANSI/NISO
Z39.48-1992 (R 1997) (Permanence of Paper).

 Michigan State University Press
East Lansing, Michigan 48823-5245

Printed and bound in the United States of America.

20 19 18 17 16 15 14   1 2 3 4 5 6 7 8 9 10

LIBRARY OF CONGRESS CATALOGING-IN-PUBLICATION DATA
Girard, René, 1923– [Quand ces choses commenceront. English]
When these things begin : conversations with Michel Treguer / René Girard ; translated
by Trevor Cribben Merrill.
pages cm. — (Studies in violence, mimesis, and culture series)
Includes bibliographical references and index.
ISBN 978-1-60917-400-2 (ebook)—ISBN 978-1-61186-110-5 (pbk. : alk. paper)
1. Girard, René, 1923—Interviews. 2. France—Intellectual life—20th century. 3.
Intellectuals—France—Interviews. I. Treguer, Michel. II. Title.
CT1018.G52A3 2014
944.084092—dc23
[B]
2013012139

Book design and composition by Charlie Sharp, Sharp Des!gns, Lansing, Michigan
Cover design by David Drummond, Salamander Design, www.salamanderhill.com
Cover art is *The Last Judgment,* altarpiece from Santa Maria degli Angioli, c. 1431
(oil on panel), Angelico, Fra (Guido di Pietro) (c. 1387–1455) / Museo di San Marco
dell'Angelico, Florence, Italy / Giraudon / The Bridgeman Art Library. Used with
permission.

g green press INITIATIVE Michigan State University Press is a member of the Green Press Initiative
and is committed to developing and encouraging ecologically responsible
publishing practices. For more information about the Green Press Initiative and the use of
recycled paper in book publishing, please visit *www.greenpressinitiative.org.*

Visit Michigan State University Press at *www.msupress.org*

Contents

Introduction

René Girard is truly an extraordinary character. He was born in 1923 in Avignon, France, but since 1947 he has lived in the United States, where he met his wife and taught for many years at Stanford University. The title of his first book—*Mensonge romantique et vérité romanesque* (1961), "Romantic Lie and Novelistic Truth," or, as the English edition would have it, *Deceit, Desire, and the Novel*—seemed innocent enough, barely hinting at the book's scandalous thesis; the essay could pass itself off as just another work of scholarly erudition, looking to unsuspecting eyes like anything but a monstrous blemish. But soon enough the veil was rent, and apocalyptic trumpets blared in the inner sanctums of our universities. At a time when most intellectuals claimed to descend from Lenin, Trotsky, or Mao, or else from Freud and Saussure, in the days when Sartre, and then Lacan, Lévi-Strauss, Althusser, Foucault, and Barthes, were still very much in vogue, strange books with incongruous titles, penned by an eccentric of the sort who usually lives in the desert, among the rattlesnakes or atop a column, started to show up on our bookstore shelves: *Violence and the Sacred* (1972), *Things Hidden since the Foundation of the World* (1978)—books that offer a general, *religious* explanation for our individual and social behavior; that consider Cervantes, Shakespeare, Marivaux, and Proust as more realistic than Marx; books that, above all, amidst the structuralist sound and fury on the Left Bank, affirm that the key to heaven has been sitting right there beneath our eyes for two thousand years, in the Gospels, where we have never dared to take hold of it, and that Jesus really is the one God incarnate that the Pope and our ultra-pious grandmothers used to tell us about. Talk about rocking the boat in which our Parisian academic discussions were taking place!

A provocation this brazen, in which new and old ideas were wantonly mixed, couldn't fail to generate reactions of the most violent sort. To be completely frank, I myself wondered whether René Girard wasn't a disciple of the terrible inquisitors or the rank-and-file missionaries who civilized so many cultures to death. I got into some lively arguments with him over the airwaves of France Culture. But there was something very strange about even these debates—the tit-for-tat and the aggressive verbal sparring that would have led any other thinker to sever ties with me once and for all left René Girard as serenely benevolent, interested, curious, amicable, and affectionate as ever. Not at all like the others, that one.

Since then, in just a few short years, the world has changed a lot. The USSR is dead. The Communist experiment has gone up in smoke, as if it had never even existed. The only alternative that philosophers were able to come up with to liberal democratic capitalism has been attempted on a truly grand scale, in real life: it didn't work. We're no longer at the same point we were at the beginning of the twentieth century, and we can no longer look forward to the "forever and forever" of centuries to come. We are blinded—or else have had our eyes opened—by History's burning paradoxes. Democracy and human rights seem to be catching on everywhere, and with everyone. It's an astonishing reversal. Here we have a system that until now was acknowledged even by its proponents to be inherently weak, incapable of measuring up to the dictatorships that remorselessly exploit their enslaved subjects—and now it appears as the most effective of all, indeed, until proven otherwise, as the only effective one. The last skeptics were reminded by the First Gulf War that the Allies of 1945 hadn't lost any of their warriors' mettle. And we can see now that the defeated parties, Germany and Japan, were able to save themselves only because they adopted the values of their conquerors. Five centuries after Columbus made his first voyage, which heralded both the spread of mercantile capitalism and the destruction of America's indigenous populations, we are meeting anew with questions that are both fascinating and frightening: the Westernization of the entire planet, the destruction of other cultures and of other systems—are these phenomena inevitable, desirable, predetermined? Is the triumph of democracy a victory for Love and Freedom, or for a mafia of gangsters who are solidifying their well-being at everyone else's expense? Are the wealthiest countries really in command of these changes, or are they themselves the playthings of planetary, physical, biological, metaphysical, and religious processes that transcend them and carry them along in their wake?

Our intellectuals have seen their idols crumble into dust and slip between their fingers. They've tried to burn them in the fire of new studies, to lose them in the immensity of new and more sophisticated paradigms, in which there is much talk of chance, self-organization, and complexity, interesting notions all, but whose very interest poorly masks an acknowledgement of helplessness when faced with the mysteries of the world.

René Girard, on the other hand, even if he keeps refining and nuancing his analyses, hasn't changed anything fundamental in his thesis, which, depending on how you look at it, can be regarded as either optimistic or apocalyptic. Some of his conclusions—the proclamation of humanity's imminent unification and uniformization—I continue to find chilling. And yet: suppose he's right? Suppose he's the one who brings *scandal* to our attention?

"We shouldn't," says Girard, "go so far as to allow good manners to prevent us from thinking."

The text that follows, transcribed and rewritten by Michel Treguer, reviewed by René Girard, is derived essentially from two recorded conversations—without anyone else present—between the authors.

However, a few pages have been taken from other sources—on the one hand, from the unpublished transcript of conversations between René Girard and Jean-Claude Guillebaud, naturally with the benevolent authorization of the latter, for which the two authors thank him—and, on the other, from texts, rewritten and reformulated, both old and new, in French and English, by René Girard.

The interlacing of themes is at once inevitable and deliberate: quite apart from the oral origin of this text, the whole of the human phenomenon discussed here can hardly be reduced to a linear exposition. Our wager is that a few repetitions won't hinder us from clearing up some of the misunderstandings that continue to surround René Girard's work.

CHAPTER 1

A First Overview:
Here and Now

MICHEL TREGUER: René, even though it may not be a very logical starting point, before laying out your thought in a more organized way, I would like to begin here and now, in the present moment in which our lives are immersed, and which, for some time now, we have seen unfurling before our eyes like a film in fast-forward. I want to do this in order to give the reader a glimpse of the immense range of applications and the tremendous interpretive power of your theory, and in order to familiarize the reader with the language we'll be speaking. Which in turn leads me to sum up in a few sentences the essential tenets of your thesis. You can correct me as we go along!

Every human group is subject to mechanisms of what you call *mimetic desire*, of imitation and reciprocal jealousy, which are ineluctable sources of violence. We each desire what others desire, and then imitate their way of desiring, and so forth. From time to time, in a more or less cyclical way, the fever of this inexorable competition culminates in a crisis that threatens the group's cohesion. This observation, which might seem merely anecdotal at first glance, is in truth the foundation of an extraordinarily powerful and far-reaching explanatory principle that makes it possible to shed light on nearly all individual and collective behavior, from domestic squabbles to large-scale historical phenomena, from the dawn of humanity to the current era.

The first societies resolved these recurrent "mimetic crises" by imputing to a victim—a *scapegoat*—the sins of the group and sacrificing it. Then, gradually, simulacra replaced the real murders: thus were born the rites of the primitive pagan religions, as well as the myths assigned the task of legitimizing them by linking them to the sacred horror of the group's origins. In other words, all human cultures are founded on murder. The initiation of children cemented these closed systems and perpetuated the power of the adults.

You think the Christian message, as it appears in the Gospels, marks an absolute break with these "eternal returns," the true beginning of a true humanity. Jesus is the first and the only one to say of myths and rituals: "These are lies, the victims were innocent. Stop envying and opposing one another, because that's the source of all evil. Love one another. Children of all nations, emancipate yourselves: your fathers are liars." In saying this, of course, he proclaims the existence of human rights, which we still hear about from time to time today, and which are thus essentially "the rights of the victims to ask for reparations from their persecutors." How does that sound to you?

RENÉ GIRARD: Fine, except when you say "your fathers are liars." Christ wouldn't have spoken like that. The rather facile condemnation of fathers was already widespread in his time, and he denounced it. He corrected the Pharisees, who said: "If we had lived at the time of our fathers, we would not have joined them in killing the prophets." The ones who talk like that are the most likely to get caught up in future mimetic escalations. The feeling of superiority they experience with respect to the past is itself a form of mimetic violence very similar to the one they think they've left behind them.

I'd like to draw particular attention to the fact that the crystallization of the group's tensions at the expense of a victim is an unconscious process. The best proof of this is that if you asked everyone today, all over France: "Do the people around you take out their frustrations on scapegoats?" everyone would answer in the affirmative; but if you then asked the same people: "And do *you* have scapegoats?" everyone would answer in the negative. To become Christian is, fundamentally, to perceive that it isn't just others who have scapegoats. And note that the two greatest Christians, the founders of the Church, Peter and Paul, were two converted persecutors. Before their conversion, they, too, thought that they didn't have any scapegoats.

Another point. Rituals aren't only, as is sometimes said, mere panto-mimes of reconciliation, a sort of harmless "happening" by which the group's members give recognition to one another and strengthen their feelings of belonging. We're talking about human culture at its strongest and most powerful. Christianity teaches us that this essential mechanism of the human condition is based on a lie, but a kind of lie that is ungraspable because of what philosophers call "the closure of representation." Each of us lives in a cultural system like a fish in a bowl. The system is closed. It is always closed, in a certain sense, by victims.

MT: Stop! Don't give too many details! We'll come back to all of these points, but it seems to me that the first thing to do is to give a broad overview of your ideas. Let me therefore add some additional remarks to my introduction, for the life and death of Christ prove insufficient to tear humanity abruptly away from the reign of hatred and lies.

On the one hand, historical Christianity ends up erring by making a "sacrificial reading" of Christ's death. Actually, you say—and even if he was treated as a scapegoat—Christ didn't die *guilty* like the victims (often divin-ized later on) of all mythical narratives, taking upon himself all of the sins of human beings, which in the end only gave them a temporary reprieve—to the contrary he was *innocent*, telling people, "From now on, live and die according to my example, without making victims, and defending victims." It is in this error that we should seek the explanation for the violence with which Christian history is tainted.

On the other hand, and more generally speaking, the revelation of this truth is a slow process that, even as it gradually eradicates these violent mechanisms, reproduces and exaggerates them along the way in all sorts of monstrous ways.

And all of this, which is already a bit complicated, brings me to my first question, which is quite simple: do you see in the recent, incredible liberation of the Eastern European countries, in an incredibly short time, the fulfillment of the promise contained in the Gospels? Are these events just another incident in twentieth century history or do they have meaning on a millennial scale?

RG: The summary that you've given of my thesis isn't, or rather is no longer, accurate. I don't say that historical Christianity is wrong. The Church does not betray the Gospels by using the word sacrifice as it does. It uses it in a sense that comes from the depths of the past, of course, but that has been renewed by what Christ does, and I don't question its legitimacy. It is the most profound meaning, the most encompassing.

In my approach there aren't the sort of radical breaks with tradition that my language has sometimes suggested. But I think we'll come back to this. As far as Marxism goes, my answer is obviously affirmative. In my view, Marxism truly does function by means of mechanisms of the "scapegoat" variety, naturally with some refinements with respect to the originary process: the victims are deliberately chosen according to a theory.

MT: The scapegoat is the bourgeoisie!

RG: Yes and no. The emergence of systems of this kind is an accident with a high probability of occurrence in the Christian world. As the truth about the mechanisms of violence gradually comes to light, secondary processes that circumvent and reduplicate them tend to arise. Marxism and Nazism are examples of such processes. From my point of view, the collapse of Marxism is the collapse of a quasi-mythical system of persecution: it is in conformity with what I see as the normal, long-term evolution of our world.

Under Stalin, the scapegoat system snowballed so much that it brings to mind a primitive society gone mad. In *The Gulag Archipelago*, for example, Solzhenitsyn recounts that the presence of a suspect in a Moscow apartment building sometimes entailed the arrest of all its occupants and sometimes of everyone living on the street. This is a little like those societies who see the birth of twins as a manifestation of violence that is contagious because it is mimetic. The members of those societies think quite "logically" that the mother must have violated some taboo, that she probably committed adultery. Sometimes the fear of violence is such that suspicion is cast on the entire family and spreads to the neighbors and everyone in the vicinity. Instead of sending everyone to the gulag, ritual purifications are carried out, which is certainly preferable. Stalinism also makes one think, *mutatis mutandis*, of the insane proliferation of human sacrifices in pre-Columbian South America.

MT: And Nazism?

RG: Our era has already lived through or is preparing to live through the collapse of the three most powerful attempts to replace religion. The collapse of Nazi Germany is the failure of a neo-paganism whose master thinkers are Nietzsche and Heidegger. The collapse of Communism is the failure of Marxism. A third collapse looms, and I hope we'll be able to avoid it: the collapse of capitalist democracies, which would be the failure of scientism, of our attempts to reduce the problems of humankind to a false objectivity, to a sort of mental and physical hygiene, in the manner of "unbridled capitalism" and psychoanalysis.

Whereas Marxism was originally based on hope, on a deviation of Christian love, Nazism is overtly anti-Christian. I think that there are presentiments of this in Nietzsche, who says clearly that, in the Christian world, it is no longer possible to make the sacrifices that according to him are indispensable; in his late period, this is what Nietzsche is really saying.

MT: Really?

RG: See for yourself: "Through Christianity, the individual was made so important, so absolute, that he could no longer be sacrificed: but the species endures only through human sacrifice . . . Genuine charity demands sacrifice for the good of the species—it is hard, it is full of self-overcoming, because it needs human sacrifice. And this pseudo humaneness called Christianity wants it established that no one should be sacrificed."[1]

The true "greatness" of National-Socialism—an expression that was actually used by Martin Heidegger in his *Introduction to Metaphysics*[2]—consisted, it seems to me, in openly combatting the project of a society without scapegoats or sacrificial victims, that is to say the Christian and modern project that Nietzsche was paradoxically the first to identify. National-Socialism seeks to render this project null and void. The idea is to deliberately go back to scapegoating, which is necessarily more criminal than archaic unconsciousness of scapegoating. Neo-paganism can lead only to that. They wanted to make a new myth by taking the Jews as victims, and they even wanted to make a new primitive myth, to go back into the German forest.

MT: Nazism is a deluded and deliberate attempt to refashion myth?

RG: Yes, in my opinion, it's a sin against the Holy Spirit. It's making victims while being aware of doing so, and for quasi-spiritual reasons, so as to close ranks at the expense of scapegoats. Marxism, to the contrary, has ultra-Christian roots!

MT: That's what I was going to say. There are flagrant resemblances between Christianity and Marxism: in both cases, there is talk, or was talk, of love, of conversion, of a Paradise to come that would spread over the entire planet. It's almost the same words, pronounced by two enemy brothers. Just now you yourself spoke of "accidents with a high probability of occurrence in the Christian world." Do you mean that the emergence of Marxism owed something to Christianity?

RG: It's deviated Christianity, to the extent that utopia necessarily fails. So, to perpetuate it, so as not to recognize the failure, there's a need for victims—in order to explain why there are still victims! And because the workers are poor and remain poor, it's the fault of the bourgeoisie, of the imperialists, and so on. You can see this logic at work even at the micro level. I remember a news story that struck me. At the beginning of the Gorbachev era, two ships collided in the Black Sea and sunk, causing a huge death toll. Whereas people in the West, in such cases, tend first to ask questions about the technical state of the ships, the signaling system, and so on, the Soviet authorities immediately asked: "Who is the guilty party?" It doesn't seem like much, but it may make it possible to understand centuries of scientific evolution and probably the technical superiority of the Christian West: mechanization as such can develop once human thought, in its attempt to come to grips with the natural world, is freed from the mechanisms of scapegoating. In a technological universe, you can't afford to replace technical causes with guilty parties. If, when a plane crashes, you're content to point the finger at the guilty party, it's quite obvious that other accidents will happen . . . And sooner or later there won't be any more planes at all!

Even if the institution of Christianity was, on a local scale, the instrument or the instigator of witch hunts, Christianity is the true destroyer of such practices, because it makes human beings aware of the arbitrary nature of the persecutory snowballing that leads to violence. It does this by way of the Passion, which is itself a persecutory escalation unveiled and condemned as such. The most remarkable thing, historically speaking, about the end of the Middle Ages, is not the epidemic of witchcraft, nor its repression, but the fact that it's the last one; it's the advent of a world in which belief in witchcraft is seen as a barely comprehensible absurdity. The idea that one shouldn't believe in this sort of thing becomes a common heritage, shared by the vast majority of people. It's no longer the exclusive and poorly-guarded privilege of a few rare emancipated individuals. Unbelief with regard to witchcraft seems to us to go without saying, so much so that we unhesitatingly point the finger on behalf of a certainty that seems natural, universally human. But where these matters are concerned, what's universally human would instead be to believe in witchcraft.

MT: Let me return to my summary. Christianity—and many of its adversaries have criticized it for this—thus really does deal a mortal blow to the specific cultures that we see disappearing every day. But, for you, this is a positive contribution. Christianity proves all cultures guilty of lying and initiates the unification of humanity. With the liberation of the Eastern Bloc countries, have we taken a giant step forward, all of a sudden?

RG: We're justified in our surprise, because, even if the process is unstoppable in the long run, it unfolds in a varied and chancy way. When people finally get around to studying the possible influence of individuals on history, they should devote a chapter to Gorbachev.

MT: In his case, one wonders if he was acting consciously or unconsciously, because you have the sense that events transformed him a great deal without his knowledge.

RG: I don't see the disappearance of cultures as a positive contribution. And I prefer to put my money on the individual and to grant Gorbachev a good dose of conscious will. Had there been another Brezhnev in his position, the whole situation might have lasted another fifty years. Totalitarian systems have a very short life expectancy: everyone realizes that the victims on which they are based are innocent; whereas, in the case of "true" myths, in pre-Christian societies, nobody realized this.

MT: The acceleration of globalization seems to lend support to what you say. It is even starting to look like there's only one possible political regime left: democracy.

RG: For centuries all human beings wanted to do was expand their horizons, and today, when the least significant news story has universal implications, when every phenomenon is global, our intellectuals turn up their noses. They assure us that "meaning is something purely local, that the real can only be grasped on a small scale." All value judgment aside, to assert that history is meaningless at the very moment that its meaning is staring us right in the face is a marvelous paradox! Ideology is dead. All that remains is the formidable difference that separates our world from all those that came before it: *today, victims have rights.* If you could talk with Greek or Roman functionaries and you tried to suggest to them that victims have rights, it wouldn't even make them laugh. They wouldn't understand. It was unthinkable in any world but our own. Whereas today this language isn't challenged by anyone. Everyone keeps saying that there are no more absolute, immutable "values" that living human beings take as self-evident—but isn't the concern for victims a value? The genius of Nietzsche made him capable of seeing that this value defines our era; but he did everything he could to fight it. All he saw in the Christian attitude was resentment, endless jeremiads, mediocre pity: it was doubtless already a little true in his era, and it's even truer today; but it isn't true at the origin, nor fundamentally: he mistook the caricature for the original. The people who defend him today talk about every Nietzsche but that one: that one is the only true, and the only, Nazi thinker. We want to forget that Nietzsche and Nazism are indissolubly linked.

MT: The unification of the planet also entails tough problems. The recent GATT agreements create a global labor market in which it may not be possible to prevent poor countries from taking jobs away from our workers, who are better paid than theirs.

RG: The same intellectuals who inveigh against the selfishness of rich countries, the insufficient aid for underdeveloped countries, and so forth, look askance at the only truly positive solution, namely the progress that these peoples are making by their own means, through sheer hard work. If there's good in capitalism, this is it. Business migrates to the countries where labor is cheap. You'll tell me that's exploitation. Probably so, but it leads to the only increases in standard of living that are actually real, rather than to a few more Mercedes-Benzes in the garages of the local bigwigs.

To prevent the exploitation of poor people, should we take the bread from their mouths and close our borders? Thanks to this excellent solution we should be able to keep making eloquent Marxist speeches while continuing to defend our privileges, without having to admit to ourselves what our true intentions are.

MT: One of the biggest paradoxes about your thesis, which we'll come back to, is that you can't actually be certain that we're really heading toward more happiness, toward the reign of love and not toward the final catastrophe.

RG: The Gospels don't in the least predict that humanity is going to choose the Reign of Love. At each crucial moment in history, humanity could take the straight and narrow path, which would involve absolutely no suffering. Today, for example, we could decide to destroy all the atomic bombs and to feed all the hungry. In theory it's possible, and in practice it's very doable. It would suffice for a few transformed people to make it happen in the most powerful countries. A good jumpstart would suffice to trigger and to propagate, *via mimetic desire*, a chain reaction. But it's a lot more likely that mimetic desire will go in the wrong direction. The law that mankind lives by on a daily basis is violence.

Apocalypse means *Revelation*, it's the same word: and from there it's easy to think that the Revelation could result in what we all mean today by the "apocalypse." The destruction of sacrificial mechanisms, in a world where science exists, where the powers of mankind are growing every day, could well mean the failure of the human adventure. It is indubitable that both the Judaic and Christian sacred texts can be read this way. But it's not my job to make prophecies. What you're asking of me, really, is a value judgment: is the world better because of the Revelation that's underway? I think it's both better and worse.

MT: Ah, I didn't expect to hear you say something like that.

RG: Don't think I'm some kind of utopian! "The Kingdom of God is not of this world." All the same, we shouldn't go to the opposite extreme, either. It is often said that our century is the worst because it has made more victims than all the others put together. This is certainly true quantitatively speaking, but there are more people on the earth than there have ever been in all of human history taken cumulatively. And it's also true that our world protects and saves more victims than any other. The two things are true at once. There is more good and more evil than ever before.

MT: But, all the same, in your mind, the balance tips in one direction more than in the other?

RG: It's not up to us to weigh good and evil. If it's history that we're trying to understand, we should be wary of placing too much importance on immediate events. What's happening today in Eastern Europe is very striking: this disturbing resurgence of a sort of tribalism, of little nationalisms, that coincides with the collapse of an ideology with universalist pretensions. But that mustn't conceal from us the true meaning of the evolution that is making way for a *global* state of affairs for which we have neither a word nor a concept: the failure of our worldviews prevents us from seeing what's universal about it.

MT: Well, I'm betting that the reader is already sufficiently intrigued by this initial overview to want to become better acquainted with your ideas—so let's return to them in a more methodical and orderly way.

CHAPTER 2

Mimetic Desire: Shakespeare rather than Plato

MT: At the beginning of your thesis there was the word "mimetic." Can you tell us again how it should be understood?

RG: Human relations are subject to conflict: whether we're talking about marriage, friendship, professional relationships, issues with neighbors or matters of national unity, human relations are always under threat.

MT: Under threat from what, by whom?

RG: . . . from the identity of desires. People influence one another and, when they're together, they have a tendency to desire the same things, primarily not because those things are rare but because, contrary to what most philosophers think, imitation also bears on desire. Humans essentially try to base their being, their profound nature and essence, on the desire of their peers.

MT: They can't desire in the absolute, so they desire by imitation? We only exist via others? There's no autonomous self?

RG: At the time I wrote *Deceit, Desire, and the Novel*, under Stendhal's influence, I contrasted mimetic desire with a "spontaneous desire." But I've gotten into the habit of using the word "desire" to refer to the various appetites, needs, and appropriations that are shot through with and governed by imitation. Mimetic phenomena interest me not only because they're present in a bunch of phenomena that seem unrelated to them, but also because using them makes it possible to think about genesis, structuration, and destructuration in a very effective way. That's why I place so much emphasis on them. But I'm not saying that they exclude all other types of explanation. For example, I believe in the love that parents have for their children, and I don't see how you could interpret that love in a mimetic fashion. I think that sexual pleasure is possible to the extent that the other is respected—and maybe there's no true satisfaction except in that case, when the shadowy presence of rivals has been banished from the lovers' bed: that's probably also why it is experienced so rarely.

I'm not saying that there's no autonomous self. I'm saying that the possibilities of the autonomous self are always hindered by mimetic desire and by a false individualism whose appetite for differences tends to have a leveling effect.

MT: All desire is religious? Even my desire for my pretty next-door neighbor?

RG: All desire is a desire for being.

MT: Why did you just say that "contrary to what most philosophers think, imitation also bears on desire"?

RG: For Plato, the real is only the imitation of distant "ideas," everything is subject to imitation except acquisitive behavior. In truth, if you take a close look at his work, *The Republic* in particular, you notice that it's haunted by the true conflict born of imitated desires, the conflict between people who are close to each other, who desire the same thing, and who all of a sudden become rivals—the sort of conflict I talk about, and that I found in the work of novelists and playwrights—but he doesn't conceptualize it.

Now if human relations are threatened by rivalries, this must have repercussions for the organization of human groups. We have a tendency to think about societies from the vantage point of their normal state, their daily functioning as it's described by very peaceful, calm people who don't think about violence. One of the great founders of political science is Hobbes, who, to a certain extent, managed to ground his thinking in crisis. He hasn't yet been entirely forgiven for that. In turn, I said to myself: if there's a normal order in society, it must be the result of a prior crisis, it must be the resolution of that crisis. And so what we have to look for and investigate is that crisis. If mimetic conflicts are contagious, in other words if there are two individuals who desire the same thing, there will soon be a third. Once there are three, four, five, six, the process starts to snowball, and everyone desires the same thing. The conflict begins with an object. But it ends up becoming so intense that it leads to the destruction or the forgetting of the object, and is transferred to the level of the antagonists who, in the absence of any real desire, become obsessed with one another. The contagion of desires gives way to that of antagonisms.

MT: Just a word about the object that's already disappeared. What was it at the start? Food?

RG: Food, land, women. When you study primitive societies, these three essential objects stand out.

MT: Now wait, let's stay politically correct. When you say "women," you're talking about the object of sexual desire. You could have spoken of men as the object of rivalry between women, no?

RG: Of course. Except that in primitive societies, it is indeed men who fight over women, because the men are stronger and have the sexual initiative.

Let me also say a word about what I call double mediation, to give you a better understanding of how the crisis escalates. Your desire, the desire I'm imitating, could have been insignificant at first, maybe it didn't even have much intensity. But when I go for the same object as you, the intensity of your desire increases. You thus become my imitator, just as I am yours. What's essential is this feedback process that makes it so that any two desires can become a sort of infernal machine. That machine produces more and more desire, more and more reciprocity, and thus more and more violence.

MT: Before coming back to the consequences of all of this for the formation of societies, let's stay on the individual level, since you were talking about novelists and playwrights: the very mechanism that you see as being at the origin of all religions and all political regimes, of history and prehistory, is also the one that we're constantly wrestling with in our daily lives, namely problems with jealousy, with love triangles (and polygons). And this is the path you started on, before coming to the more general questions with which we began.

RG: Yes, exactly. I'd noticed that in writers like Stendhal and Proust the same geometry governed human relations even though they were describing different worlds. Then I found the same forces at work in Cervantes, Shakespeare, Molière, Marivaux, Dostoevsky, Joyce, and so on. Not to mention cases that are almost too obvious like *Carmen* over which we throw the hypocritical veil of "bad taste": "If you don't love me, I love you! If I love you, you'd better watch out!" It's too obvious. At the end, the counterpoint between the bullfight and the execution of the victim—it's facile, of course, but it's also magnificent. When works of art are so hugely successful, there are profound reasons for it.

And ask yourself why this colossus of desire and conflicts that's called *The Ring* begins with scenes of grotesque marivaudage, the amorous provocations of the three Rhine maidens? It's a visionary beginning, straight out of Marivaux, but also straight out of Shakespeare. The gold is *nothing*, clearly, since it's the ray of sunshine that alights on it and transfigures it. And yet the gold is *everything*, since it's what everyone is fighting over; it's the fact of fighting over it that gives it its value, and its terror.

Little by little it became apparent to me that psychoanalytic suspicion didn't go far enough. Freud's sham "radicalism" ceased to impress me, and I understood that what the critics have always disdained in novelistic works— the recurrence of fascination and jealousy, the reciprocal manipulations, the lies aimed at others or at oneself, and so forth—everything that they disparagingly group under the heading "literary psychology" or "amorous scheming," everything that puts off their delicate aestheticism by its repetitive character, are the fundamental maneuvers and ruses of mimetic desire: what Proust rightly calls "psychological laws."

Only the great writers succeed in portraying these mechanisms without distorting them to spare their egos: here we have a system of relationships that paradoxically, or rather not paradoxically at all, is less variable the greater a writer is. "Psychology" really is a matter of laws, and the aesthetes don't want to see it because they only appreciate the singular, the supremely original or, in our day and age, "differences," which are the same thing democratized. Contemporary aesthetic sensibility is still the prisoner of romantic conceptions.

MT: These days you're more likely to cite Shakespeare, to whom you devoted a book.

RG: Shakespeare's first works are haunted by the following insight: friendship and hatred go hand in hand, best friends are also the ones most threatened by ferocious enmity. Take the two gentlemen of Verona: they've always lived together, they imitate each other in every way, they like each other, they adore each other, neither of them can do without the other; and, suddenly, amorous rivalry strikes, like lightning, as a mere variant of that same imitation. I think that all the excessively optimistic attitudes we have about human beings hide the following truth from us: *in human relations there is a conflict principle that can't be resolved by rational means.* The conflict between rivals in love, or between two ambitious rivals, will never be healed by an idea or by recalling the distant past.

My Bible of mimetic desire is *Troilus and Cressida*, but I first discovered Shakespeare through *A Midsummer Night's Dream*. From a literary standpoint, it's the best memory of my life. I first saw the play on television. I didn't completely understand it because I hadn't read it. But I was ready to read it: I had developed the whole hypothesis of mimetic desire, and suddenly I found it in Shakespeare in its most complete form, with direct anthropological repercussions. *A Midsummer Night's Dream* is in the first place a comprehensive treatise on mimetic desire, which concerns four lovers but eventually leads all the way to the violent destruction of society. In a few pages, we're taken from the most ridiculous rivalries—boyfriends and girlfriends without any personality who flirt with and imitate each other—to the production of mythological monsters. *A Midsummer Night's Dream* verified for me the truth of the itinerary that had led me from Marivaux to sacrifice, and it did so in magnificent language, with incomparable poetry. In the play you find literal definitions of mimetic desire, formulations like: "O hell! to choose love by another's eye!"

Then, in *Troilus and Cressida*, I turned up: "It's mad idolatry when the service is greater than the god." Idolatry is the fascination exerted on us by a human being who doesn't deserve so much devotion. It's the war, the mimetic rivalry that drives Helen's value up to insane heights, transforming her into an idol in the eyes of the Greeks but also the Trojans.

MT: I think we can now begin to understand why some academics turn up their noses in disgust when faced with the ramifications of your hypothesis: not only do you lead them back to church, where they haven't set foot in ages, but you've also dragged them out of the conference room, with its polite discussions, and into the bedroom.

RG: Joyce recounts a scene like that in *Ulysses*. Stephen Dedalus (who is Joyce's double) is giving a brilliant lecture on Shakespeare, in whose works he discovers, in my view, the mimetic mechanism. And a critic stands up and says: "You have brought us all this way to show us a French triangle?" In other words, "All this talk just to bring Shakespeare down to the level of some vaudeville love triangle?" And the contradictor adds: "Do you believe your own theory?" Petrified, Dedalus says: "No." Even today, the critics think this is the acknowledgment that the mimetic Shakespeare is a joke, without any relation to the truth. But, ten lines later, Dedalus murmurs: "I believe, O Lord, help my unbelief!" It's a phrase from the Gospels, spoken by the father of a healed child, and it means "strengthen my desire to believe," to believe in God for the speaker in the Gospels, and in the divinized Self in the case of Dedalus-Joyce. As soon as Dedalus is alone, his theory is reborn, his theology of the Self reemerges. But in the moment, among the group, he is mimetically crushed. And right afterwards you have these incredible sentences: "Who helps to believe?" "Egomen" (the self). "Who to unbelieve?" "Other chap,"[1] the other. Everything is there, in three lines. How can you expect a hurried reader to understand Joyce? It took me a year and a half to unpack this text. And the "French triangle"! I can't tell you how many people in the United States have told me: "Mimetic desire is interesting, but it only works for French literature, it's a French thing." Joyce had obviously had the same experience.

MT: Joyce is talking about himself through Dedalus and Shakespeare?

RG: In this text he's complaining indirectly about having been hounded from Ireland by the lack of understanding he faced in his intellectual milieu.

MT: You've even said that Joyce had to avoid being understood in order to prove that he was right.

RG: The text portrays incomprehension, and that incomprehension is reproduced and mirrored in current literary criticism. Thus to understand the text, you have to understand it in a context of incomprehension that was deliberately perpetuated by Joyce himself. It begins with the lecture, Dedalus's reading of Shakespeare: to understand the mimetic Shakespeare, you have to be as mimetic as him. But the text about Shakespeare is a mise en abyme of *Ulysses*, of the entire novel. Joyce is saying to his critics: "You're all blind, you don't understand Shakespeare. I'm just as mimetic as him, I share his sickness and I share his genius." He's trying to establish a more or less secret complicity between himself and Shakespeare. It's pretty incredible!

One of his listeners says scornfully to Dedalus: "You're doing petty biographical criticism?" And he cites Villiers de l'Isle-Adam, who said: "Let's leave the writer's life to his servants, and speak only of literature." The fake avant-garde derealizes literature, whereas Joyce, to the contrary, is secretly saying: "*Ulysses* is my experience, it's my life." Joyce couldn't care less about the avant-gardist literary values that are ascribed to him. Indeed, his letters to Nora contain the entirety of Dostoevsky's *Eternal Husband*, which is to say a model of mimetic literature. He displays obsessive jealousy toward a fellow who had courted Nora (before Joyce) and who died of an illness.

It's this death that heightens to a maximum the ordeal of rivalry, to the extent that the rival, once dead, is invulnerable; it's a situation from *The Eternal Husband*. What's most amazing is that Joyce is totally unaware that he's repeating in both his work and his life Dostoevsky's work and life (and correspondence). What he sees in Shakespeare's case he doesn't see in Dostoevsky's.

MT: I'll leave our readers to imagine for themselves the personal echoes that René Girard, who has revealed Joyce to us in this new light and who has himself written a book on Shakespeare, may hear resonating in this analysis. To come back to the philosophers—you think the novelists are ultimately much more profound than they are?

RG: I don't want to say anything bad about philosophers . . . or at least nothing too bad! In Plato's particular case there is something respectable in his determination not to open the mimetic wound: it seems to me that he's afraid of aggravating it by its mere mention. In an era when Christianity didn't yet exist, to say "ideas don't play nearly as great a role as you think they do in stirring up the major human conflicts" could lead only to a form of cynicism, even nihilism; I can thus understand his scruples.

MT: You make me think of Dante, who saves Virgil and a few others from the Inferno, "because, being born before Christ, they couldn't have known. . . ."

RG: It's true that I'm not as indulgent with modern philosophers like Nietzsche and Heidegger. But maybe I'm wrong. I'm not condemning anyone. Everything I put forward is exploratory and tentative in nature.

CHAPTER 3

The Mimetic Crisis: Sacrificial Worlds

MT: Let's go back to the formation of societies. We were talking about the moment when the escalation of the mimetic crisis leads to a "contagion of antagonisms."

RG: Inasmuch as they desire the same thing, the members of the group become antagonists, in pairs, in triangles, in polygons, in whatever configurations you can imagine. The contagion signifies that some of them are going to abandon their personal antagonist and "choose" their neighbor's. We see this all the time, when, for example, we shift the hatred we feel for our private enemies, but that we don't dare take out against them, onto politicians. In this way partial scapegoats emerge, and by means of the same phenomenon they are gradually reduced in number even as their symbolic charge intensifies.

MT: The crisis becomes more and more unbearable, it's impossible to go on like that, a solution must be found.

RG: I don't really like your formulation: "a solution *must* be found." It makes it sound like the discovery of the scapegoat is a deliberate act. This is what a lot of misleading summaries of my thesis say. In primitive societies, the process only reaches consciousness in the guise of the sacred. Even now, it is mostly unconscious.

MT: We prefer to think that everything can be blamed on a single individual.

RG: We don't "prefer" it, we truly think that the scapegoat is guilty. Because of their mimetic predisposition, thinking this way comes "quite naturally" to human beings.

MT: That's very interesting, it "resonates" with many other innovative currents of cutting-edge thought that are grappling with complex phenomena, with "sensitivity to initial conditions," the enormous and unpredictable consequences of microscopic events, "strange attractors," "fractals," the global indeterminacy of phenomena that are nonetheless governed on a local scale by deterministic equations, and so on. Already, the clumping of tensions around scapegoats that are less and less partial makes one think of the birth of tornadoes or of lumps in a composite mixture. But, what's more, in the "designation" of the collective victim, we now see chance at work—the same chance that physicists, paleontologists, and others find so interesting. And I suspect that the question of democracy must not be far behind.

RG: We're talking about order being born from disorder, which in current epistemology is really the highlight of the whole process, the showstopping act. There's no more enemy, there's no more vengeance, because the absolute enemy has been put to death in the person of the scapegoat. If the reconciliation is strong enough, if the misfortune and suffering that preceded it were great enough, the shock is such that the community wonders about its good fortune. It's too modest to give itself credit. It knows from experience that it is incapable of overcoming its divisions by its own means, incapable of patching together its own *social contract*, if you will. It thus turns once more to its scapegoat. It makes the scapegoat itself responsible for its efficiency as a scapegoat. To the idea that the scapegoat can destroy the community is now added the idea that it can rebuild the community. This is the invention of the *sacred*, which early ethnology understood to be present in all cultures.

Sacralization makes the victim the model of a strictly religious imitation and counter-imitation. The victim is asked to help the community protect its reconciliation, so it won't fall back into the crisis of rivalry. Everyone thus takes care not to imitate whatever the victim did, or appeared to do, to trigger the crisis: potential antagonists avoid each other and are separated from each other. They undertake not to desire the same objects. Measures are taken to avoid the same generalized mimetic contagion; the group divides itself up and separates its members by means of *taboos*.

When crisis appears to be looming once more, the group resorts to drastic measures and imitates what the victim did, or seemed to do, to save the community. The victim allowed itself to be killed. Therefore a victim is chosen as a substitute, and dies in the original victim's place, a *sacrificial* victim: this is the invention of *ritual*. Finally, the sacred visitation is remembered: this is called *myth*. Mythological monsters bear witness to the disorder that leaves its trace on these narratives, which spring from representational distortions at the time of the mimetic crisis.

In sacrifice, myth is remade. So that the scapegoat mechanism works anew and reestablishes the group's unity once again, great care is taken to copy the original sequence very exactly. The first step is thus to plunge the group deliberately into an imitation of the mimetic crisis.

Ethnologists have never understood why, in their rituals, so many communities deliberately unleash the type of crisis that they fear the most. They do it to arrive faster at the immolation of the victim, which, it is thought, will bring back order and peace once more.

Once you understand this, you see that founding myths refer to founding violence. They actually recount it. The reason ethnologists never spot the scapegoat is because the process is depicted by persecutors who are its playthings, persecutors who are convinced of their violence's legitimacy, and their victim's guilt.

Many ethnologists, classicists, and theologians have, they say, opened their eyes wide, and yet they don't see the scapegoat in myths. They don't understand what I'm saying. They don't realize that, for me, the scapegoat is not a theme but a source of illusion that engenders an essentially deceptive text. An illusion cannot appear as such, by definition, in the text it engenders. They don't recognize Oedipus for the scapegoat he is.

MT: I was going to ask you to give us a concrete demonstration using a myth that everyone is familiar with. Let's recall that the drama unfolds in Thebes, from which the young Oedipus—son of King Laius and Queen Jocasta—has been sent away because the oracle predicted that he would kill his father and marry his mother. But Oedipus, who was miraculously saved as a child, once he is an adult, happens to kill a passerby without knowing that it's his father and, as a reward for having solved the Sphinx's riddles, is given the Queen's hand in marriage. He discovers the horror of his fate even as the plague begins to ravage Thebes, and then he puts out his eyes, and, banished by his sons, wanders in exile guided by his daughter Antigone.

But isn't it true that, even if he did so involuntarily and without realizing it, Oedipus really *did* kill his father and marry his mother? And is there any link between his fate and the plague?

RG: I'm pleased with this objection, because it's the number one misunderstanding about the nature of my thesis. People think that I'm interpreting themes just as they appear, and they miss the extreme radicalism of what I'm doing. I don't hesitate to contradict the text, just as we contradict witch hunters when they assure us that their victims are really guilty. Myth must be demolished in the same way that we demolish witch trials. It must be shown that, behind myth, there is neither pure imagination nor a pure event but an account that has been distorted by the efficiency of the scapegoat mechanism itself, a mechanism that myth tells about in all sincerity but that is necessarily transfigured by the tellers, who are the persecutors.

The theme of the individual who gives the plague to his community because he committed parricide and incest—doesn't it trouble you a little, doesn't it arouse your suspicions? Do you believe that this theme is true, or do you think that it's been invented? Neither the one nor the other in my opinion. It's an accusation that's typical of collective lynching in a period of crisis, a plague period. It cannot appear otherwise than it does in the myth since it comes from the unanimous persecutors and not from the victim.

We would know at once what we were dealing with if the text of the myth was presented in a Western, historical context, a medieval context for example. We have a panicked community on our hands that has embarked on a scapegoat-hunt and has mimetically polarized itself against the most prestigious and also the most envied citizen of all. In a sense, nothing could be more "normal" than the transformation of a king into a scapegoat.

We have to stop having so much reverence for the mythical text. The great number of myths that reproduce the same structure starting with different but analogous accusations makes the mimetic reading almost as obvious as the reality and injustice of the witch hunts of the fifteenth century. Sooner or later—you'll see the day, but I won't—people will understand that I'm right.

To grasp this kind of myth, you have to ask yourself how a panicked lynch mob would react if, after their arbitrary lynching, you asked them about what they had just done. They would describe not the arbitrary violence to which they had succumbed, not the truth about their act, but the myth such as we know it today, or a variant of the same lie. They would tell you that for legitimate reasons they hounded from the community an individual who had really committed the fantastic crimes of which he was accused. They would tell you that he's the king who gave them the plague because he really did kill his father and sleep with his mother.

In the parts of the globe where crowd phenomena remain violent, myths analogous to the Oedipus myth are reinvented every day. The greatest novelist of the American South, William Faulkner, understood this.

Oedipus is the scapegoat in *Oedipus the King*, and, like all good ancient scapegoats, he is transformed into a sort of divinity. The other play by Sophocles that deals with Oedipus, *Oedipus at Colonus*, is all about Oedipus divinized. To make gods by expelling and, most often, killing them, is the quintessential human gesture.

MT: There remains a stage that we haven't yet mentioned: when the victim is already sacred before it is killed.

RG: It's a stage that's already ritualized, beyond the founding murder. It's the birth of royalty. Ritual imitation can lead to sacrifice properly speaking or to what is called royalty.

MT: You even say: "Royalty is when the victim comes to power."

RG: It's just an expression, of course, but there are indeed many societies in which it's the king who ends up getting sacrificed. As for how that happens, why some systems tip in the direction of a king and give themselves a sacred central power, and why others maintain dual institutions—it's impossible to say in detail. It's a result of the unpredictable interplay of the little, disorderly fluctuations that you were talking about earlier, from which order nonetheless emerges.

MT: In hearing you describe these mimetic crises, I can't keep from asking myself once again: is what he's telling me true, did it really, physically happen, or is it just a nice story, a way of looking at things?

RG: I think it's more than just a way of looking at things, but the real crises, as a rule, must lack the clarity of the crises portrayed by the Greek tragedians or by the rites that preceded theater. What is true is the real victim; the emissary mechanism requires a real victim. I don't think we can say anything more. But don't lose sight of the efficiency of the mimetic hypothesis, of its explanatory power.

MT: I'm not forgetting the numerous echoes that I hear resonating from other disciplines. Is there any point in trying to situate these events historically? In the Paleolithic or the Neolithic Age?

RG: Hominization can be imagined as extending over hundreds of thousands or millions of years. What makes humankind specific is "symbolicity," that is to say the ability to have a system of thought that makes it possible to hand a culture down from generation to generation. And that can only begin with the victim and sacrifice. Or more exactly, beyond the victim, with taboos on the one hand and ritual imitation on the other.

MT: A group of rites linked to a language engender a "system of representation," a worldview, and form a culture.

RG: A certain specialization, a differentiation of functions is spontaneously developed due to innumerable sacrificial repetitions of the founding murder. Certain sacrifices prefigure initiation rites, others funerary rites, and still others marriage rites. We necessarily have a tendency to read this link backwards, starting with the endpoint: to believe that it's the need for funerals, for education, that is fruitful, and that religion is added on. There are fundamentally only two ways of looking at religion: as superfluous, added on—or as the origin of everything.

MT: Moving on. According to you, all cultures are based on murder and deceit: but why shouldn't there just be a social contract, a voluntary agreement among the members of the group?

RG: Because mimetic rivalries stand in the way! All the philosophers locate society's origin in a deliberate decision, but one that, all the same, is born of a sort of constraint: the need to come to an agreement on certain things. In the end this is even true of Hobbes, who, lacking the scapegoat mechanism, must conclude: violence looms, thus human beings are obliged to collaborate. It's even true of Freud, in *Totem and Taboo*: first there's the murder of the father, and then the brothers fight, and one fine day they decide to make peace. And so they sit down at the negotiating table. It's this idea of a well-thought-out starting point that I'm against. Durkheim is just about the only one who truly senses that society couldn't have started like that, when he talks about initial "effervescence." But then he's wrong to give the great Australian rites as an example of effervescence: that's assuming the conclusion in the premises. That's why I locate the effervescence before ritual and give as its origin mimetic rivalry, which is already there at the animal stage. Human society begins from the moment symbolic institutions are created around the victim, that is to say when the victim becomes sacred.

Academics and bureaucrats are the only ones who think that everything always begins with committees.

MT: Could it be said that, in the tribal world where it was born, Christianity invented the individual soul, or the individual subject, or simply the individual, period?

RG: I think Christianity pushed the discovery of the person as far as it could go, but the term used is of little importance. That discovery is one and the same as the loosening of ritual constraints, as the desacralization of the social.

Like all great Christian innovations, this one is vulnerable to terrifying distortions and perversions. The modern individual is what remains of the person when romantic ideologies have finished with it, it's an idolatry of self-sufficiency that is necessarily deceptive, an anti-mimetic philosophy of the will that immediately causes a redoubling of imitation, an ever more complete submission to the group, which is itself ever more subject to the futile pull of fashion, and thus always exposed to totalitarian temptations.

CHAPTER 4

The Bible

MT: We're making our way toward the great historical rupture, the creation of History itself, that you see the word of Christ as opening up. But don't you think it would be a good idea to stop and talk about the Bible?

RG: Yes. One senses that the Bible is heading toward Revelation properly speaking in the New Testament.

In the most primitive pagan myths, sacrifice and murder do not seek to hide themselves. They naively expose themselves, in all candor one might say. That is why they are so transparent, why they make it easy to guess at the existence of the scapegoat system.

As for Plato, whom we were talking about, he's past that stage. He looks at the myth of Chronos, observes that all of the violence has been heaped on him, that he's been made into a kind of ogre, and he says: "We mustn't tell such abominable stories to little children; either it's a joke, and it should be completely forgotten, or else it's true, in which case it should be reserved for a very prudent elite able to understand these things; and, in the latter case, we'll take the precaution of covering ourselves with a major sacrifice, the sacrifice of a horse, for example."[1] What is Plato doing? He's seeking to suppress the last traces of violence, but always by sacrificial means: it's like

Lady Macbeth washing her hands, or Pilate, it's the opposite of Revelation. It's not the highlighting of truth, it's a new cover-up of violence by violence.

The principle, the goal of philosophy, of humanism, is to hide the founding murder. To be Christian is to unveil it.

The Bible, on the other hand, is moving toward the light. Leviticus 19 begins with a whole series of negative propositions: "You will not go about slandering your own family; nor will you put your neighbor's life in jeopardy," "You will not harbor hatred for your brother." And then the positive reversal surges forth, all at once, like a lightning bolt: "You will love your neighbor as yourself."

What the Gospels add is that they describe the entire scapegoat system. Starting with the word "scandal" or starting with the word "Satan," you see the whole imitative thread unwind, from the individual all the way up to the collective scale. The Passion narrative is essential because it reveals the mimetic process of founding murders.

But there are already many texts in the Bible, notably in the historical books, in Judges, that are narrative retellings of myths from a demystifying point of view. Even in Genesis, compare the story of Joseph with the Oedipus myth. In both cases you first have a baby who constitutes a threat to his family. The oracle says that Oedipus will kill his father and marry his mother, and Joseph has dreams in which he reigns over his brothers. The brothers get rid of Joseph in the same way as the father and mother get rid of Oedipus. In the second part, the child has been saved and, now adult, he commits a crime or appears to commit one, the rape of Potiphar's wife in Joseph's case, parricide and incest in Oedipus's. In both texts the hero finds himself associated with a terrible social scourge: drought on the one hand, the plague on the other. And the true question that both texts ask is: is he guilty? To this question the pagan myth always answers: "Yes, Oedipus is guilty, yes he is a threat to his father and mother, yes he committed patricide and incest, yes he's the one who is responsible for the plague, he must be punished." Whereas the Biblical texts answer: "No, the twelve hypocritical brothers and the Egyptians are peddling lies about Joseph, making him into a scapegoat. In reality, Joseph is innocent." Where the myth sees the scapegoat as "the true culprit," the story of Joseph sees an innocent party wrongly convicted.

If you keep my subversive reading of Oedipus in mind, a reading that recognizes a falsely legitimate system of accusation in myth, you'll have no trouble seeing that the story of Joseph does the opposite of the myth. Just as there is behind the myth a scapegoat mechanism that's fully functional and that we don't see, because we accept the guilt of Oedipus at face value—as you did yourself—so behind the Joseph story there must be a myth that, while not exactly the Oedipus myth, is very similar, and is consistently reworked and contradicted by the Biblical narrative. This contradiction consistently works in favor of the accused. This reworking has great value for the interpretation of the myth and for the reinstatement of the truth violated by the scapegoat mechanism. The story of Joseph is quintessentially Biblical in the sense of a rectification of what had been twisted to the victim's detriment.

The last part of the text confirms my idea, insofar as it explicitly reveals the vital role played throughout all of history by the question of the scapegoat. Having become Grand Vizier of Egypt, Joseph resupplies his hungry brothers, who have come to ask for his help and who don't recognize him beneath his sumptuous Egyptian garments. To put them to the test, to see if, once again, they will expel one of their brothers as they once expelled him, Joseph arranges to falsely accuse the youngest, Benjamin: he keeps him prisoner and gives the elder brothers permission to go away. They all decide to leave, with the exception of Judah, who offers to become Joseph's prisoner in his brother's stead.

The mere fact that Judah refuses the scapegoat system is enough to move Joseph, who reveals his identity to his brothers and forgives them all.

When Christians perceive in Joseph and above all in Judah a Christ figure, a *figura Christi*, they're not the simpletons imagined by the half-clever purveyors of pseudo-scientific criticism. There really is a close relationship between Christ's attitude and Judah's gesture of agreeing to be the scapegoat so that his brother won't be.

MT: As they say at concerts: encore!

RG: Another example is the story of Job, who is perhaps the first to truly throw the sacrificial system out of whack. Job is sick, and he has a bunch of victimary signs: he is covered in pustules, people throw rocks at him, even his wife tells him he has bad breath and rejects him. He's lost his herds, and he sows contagious disorder all around him. He's the archetypal victim. His three friends tell him, as a sort of consolation I suppose: "Since bad things are happening to you, you must be guilty. Repent." That's pagan theology in a nutshell. But Job resists and tries to subvert the system of the emissary victim. Job's friends represent the crowd arrayed against the victim, the mythical perspective. Truth is fighting against myth. At the beginning of the story, God says to Satan: "You'll see, Job won't speak against me." Later, he seems to do so, but in fact he is speaking against a god of violence who is neither the Yahweh of the prophets nor the Father to whom Jesus refers.

MT: Job resists the guilty verdict?

RG: He resists, and in doing so, he moves—perhaps coming close to atheism—toward a religion in which God has no solidarity with vengeful crowds. The text is an implicit critique of the theology that saw those excluded by human beings as ostracized by God. Instead of saying, as Oedipus did, "Okay, the one who killed his father and slept with his mother is me, banish me, I'm a piece of dirt," Job stands up and says: "No way! Your oracles are lies! If that's what Apollo is all about, then I don't want anything to do with him!" That's something the Greeks could never say. And that's where the fundamental distinction lies.

CHAPTER 5

Christ (Orders and Disorders)

MT: In your view, Christian revelation triggers a process that is global, worldwide or perhaps even wider. We emerge from the lie, from the mythical shadow, and are reborn under the sun of truth. It's the beginning of History as such, and it's not just one more myth.

RG: From a Christian point of view, it could be said that, in a sense, Creation starts up again. Creation damaged by sin.

MT: What sin exactly?

RG: Mankind's sin, original sin.

MT: Yes, but how do you define it?

RG: I don't presume to define it, but I'm saying that the mimetic system is a big part of it. Original sin begins on an individual level in Genesis, with Adam and Eve, but it immediately continues on the group level with Cain and Abel: the murder of the brother, you see, is the creation of human culture. The whole mimetic system is there, and the Gospels say so, I think.

They have Jesus say that "he is going to die like the prophets" and, among the prophets, Abel is mentioned. That shows that it's not only a question of the Jewish prophets, but of all religious murders since the foundation of the world, murders that all resemble the Passion inasmuch as they are all founding murders in the scapegoat sense. The death of Christ occurs in continuity with those murders. What's unique about the Passion is not the way in which Christ dies—how could crucifixion be unique given that it's the most common torture in the Roman world?—it's that, instead of ending with a sacralization of the scapegoat, it ends with a *desacralization* of the whole system. And what Christianity says, which is obviously very paradoxical, is that this Revelation which desacralizes everything is the only truly religious one, the only one that is truly divine.

Structurally, the Gospels resemble a myth: there's a crisis, there's a collective murder, there's a religious revelation. In order to understand that it's not the same thing, it's necessary to look at what is said about the victim. It's not at all the same thing to look at a murder from the vantage point of the murderers as it is to look at it from the vantage point of the innocent victim.

MT: One could make the following objection: given that the mythical text obviously doesn't acknowledge its lie, your assertion that this text is lying and that the Gospel text is speaking the truth necessarily comes before any sort of analysis; your system of representation and that of your critics are both closed, mutually exclusive. Discussion is impossible.

RG: An excellent objection, and one that sums up many others. But my response is that it isn't true that I assume a priori that myths are lies and the Gospel is the truth. To the contrary, it's the modern world and its pseudo-science that, without any serious reflection, takes as a given that everything is mythical, including the Passion, that everything is false. By resisting the mimetic escalation that myths fail to resist, the Gospels identify, penetrate, and explain that to which myth is too completely subject even to see. The Gospels see that Oedipus's guilt—like Christ's—is a panicked crowd's "frame-up job," they are able to describe what pagan eyes think they see, the scapegoat first killed and then later falsely divinized as the source of reconciliation.

The Gospel of Luke says that "and though Herod and Pilate had been enemies before, they were reconciled that same day." It's a reconciliation that obviously isn't Christian, but rather the result of the sacrifice for those who believe in it. And even more striking: Herod believes in the resurrection of John the Baptist, whose killing he ordered! It's written (Matthew 14:2)! Of Jesus, whose fame has spread all the way to him, the panic-stricken tetrarch declares: "This man is John the Baptist! It's him, risen from the dead; that's why he possesses the power to work miracles!" Herod divinizes his victim as a scapegoat, insofar as he killed him.

The Gospels see that myth is dominated by a false accusation, while myth can tell us nothing about the Gospels. Without Gospel intelligence we see only the proximity of mythical and evangelical themes, "diabolical" resemblance, Satan's "aping," which gives us to believe that it's the same thing everywhere. But the vantage point of the murderers, even if they are "innocently" and sincerely intoxicated by their murder, and ultimately grateful to their victim for having "saved" them, isn't worth the victim's truth, which proves capable of analyzing and explaining everything. That truth, on the other hand, cannot be analyzed and explained by solely human means. Christ is not divinized as a scapegoat. Those who hold him to be God— Christians—are those who do not make him their scapegoat.

MT: Myths justify violence, but the rites that they engender also stop violence?

RG: Myths justify violence against the scapegoat, the community is never guilty. Thebes isn't guilty with respect to Oedipus, Oedipus is guilty with respect to Thebes. But ritual protects communities from the great violence of mimetic disorder thanks to the real and symbolic violence of sacrifice. To use Jean-Pierre Dupuy's expression, "sacrificial systems *contain* violence, in both senses of the word": because violence is inside them, and because they prevent it from submerging everything.

MT: But after all, maybe it's not so bad to contain violence like that, by "mediating" it through rites?

RG: It's not so bad, but violence always comes back.

MT: But at minimum cost.

RG: Maybe at minimum cost, but also at the cost of the truth, by the grace of deceit. Some primitive societies avoid striking out at the true guilty party because it might awaken the spirit of vengeance. Channeling violence toward a sacrificial victim as if toward a lightning rod doubtless stops violence, but it's not very pretty. Even if we are very selective about what arouses our indignation, and sometimes very hypocritical, it remains true to say that, on the whole, we no longer tolerate that solution.

MT: We can't condemn sacrifice, because it is unconscious, but we cannot recommend it because, as we were saying earlier, if we carry it out knowingly, it becomes Nazism.

RG: Making sacrifice into an ideology leads to awful things.

MT: On the other hand, what happens before the emergence of Christianity isn't "evil." It's just human history, no?

RG: It's human history. But the Bible is better, it resists the scapegoat phenomenon. Prior religions are completely submerged in the sacrificial universe, subject to its mechanisms, but with a certain innocence. Actually, the word *innocence* is dangerous and excessive; in the Acts of the Apostles, there's an extraordinary text that speaks of *ignorance*. Peter walks toward the crowd in Jerusalem and says: "You don't realize what you have done, you've killed the son of God, and you didn't know it, you didn't understand, even your leaders were unaware." That is to say that he grants even to the cynical politicians, to Caiaphas and Pilate, the benefit of unconsciousness: their little schemes didn't touch upon the essential.

MT: That also makes me think of Jesus's "Father, forgive them for they know not what they do." And yet, doesn't Christ also speak of violence?

RG: "I didn't come to bring peace but war, I came to separate the son from the father, the daughter from the mother, and so on" doesn't mean, "I've come to bring violence," but rather, "I've come to bring a kind of peace that is so utterly free of victims that it surpasses what you are capable of and eventually you'll have to come to a reckoning with your victimary phenomena." These texts are the religious texts of the modern world. They're not just Western. They don't belong to anyone, they're universal.

MT: The arrival of Christ disturbs the sacrificial order, the cycle of little false periods of temporary peace following sacrifices?

RG: The story of the "demons of Gerasa" in the synoptic Gospels, and notably in Mark, shows this well. To free himself from the crowd that surrounds him, Christ gets on a boat, crosses Lake Tiberias, and comes to shore in non-Jewish territory, in the land of the Gerasenes. It's the only time the Gospels venture among a people who don't read the Bible or acknowledge Mosaic law. As Jesus is getting off the boat, a possessed man blocks his way, like the Sphinx blocking Oedipus. "The man lived in the tombs and no one could secure him anymore, even with a chain. All night and all day, among the tombs and in the mountains, he would howl and gash himself with stones." Christ asks him his name, and he replies: "My name is Legion, for there are many of us." The man then asks, or rather the demons who speak through him ask Christ not to send them out of the area—a telling detail—and to let them enter a herd of swine that happen to be passing by. And the swine hurl themselves off the edge of the cliff into the lake. It's not the victim who throws himself off the cliff, it's the crowd. *The expulsion of the violent crowd is substituted for the expulsion of the single victim.* The possessed man is healed and wants to follow Christ, but Christ tells him to stay put. And the Gerasenes come en masse to beg Jesus to leave immediately. They're pagans who function thanks to their expelled victims, and Christ is subverting their system, spreading confusion that recalls the unrest in today's world. They're basically telling him: "We'd rather continue with our exorcists, because you, you're obviously a true revolutionary. Instead of reorganizing the demoniac, rearranging it a bit, like a psychoanalyst, you do away with it entirely. If you stayed, you would deprive us of the sacrificial crutches that make it possible for us to get around." That's when Jesus says to the man he's just liberated from his demons: "You're going to explain it to them." It's actually quite a bit like the conversion of Paul. Who's to say that historical Christianity isn't a system that, for a long time, has tempered the message and made it possible to wait for two thousand years? Of course this text is dated because of its primitive demonological framework, but it contains the capital idea that, in the sacrificial universe that is the norm for mankind, Christ always comes too early. More precisely, Christ must come when it's time, and not before. In Cana he says: "My hour has not come yet." This theme is linked to the sacrificial crisis: Christ intervenes at the moment the sacrificial system is complete.

This possessed man who keeps gashing himself with stones, as Jean Starobinski has revealed, is a victim of "auto-lapidation." It's the crowd's role to throw stones. So, it's the demons of the crowd that are in him. That's why he's called *Legion*—in a way he's the embodiment of the crowd. It's the crowd that comes out of him and goes and throws itself off of the cliff. We're witnessing the birth of an individual capable of escaping the fatal destiny of collective violence.

MT: These texts are at one and the same time very beautiful and obscure; they need to be explicated, clarified. "What is hidden will be revealed." Why must Revelation be hidden?

RG: It's not that it *must* be hidden, actually it's not hidden at all. It's mankind that is blind. We're inside the closure of representation, everyone is in the fishbowl of his or her culture. In other words, mankind doesn't see what I was saying earlier, the principle of illusion that governs our viewpoint. Even after the Revelation, we still don't understand.

MT: Does that mean that things are going to emerge gradually, but that at first they're incomprehensible?

RG: They seem incomprehensible because mankind lives under the sign of Satan, lives a lie and lives in fear of the lie, in fear of liars. The reversal performed by the Passion has yet to occur.

MT: Insofar as the Church itself has been mistaken for two thousand years and has been practicing a sacrificial reading of the Passion of the Christ, that reading is a way of hiding Revelation.

RG: I'm not saying that the Church is mistaken. The reading that I'm proposing is in line with all the great dogmas, but it endows them with an anthropological underpinning that had gone unnoticed.

MT: Why not just clean up our bad habits by sweeping them away once and for all in the year zero, making way for an era of love and infinite peace?

RG: Because the world wouldn't have been able to take it! Since the sacrificial principle is the fundamental principle of the human order—up to a certain point human beings need to pour out their violence and tensions onto scapegoats—destroying it all at once is impossible. That's why Christianity is made in such a way as to allow for transitions. This is no doubt one of the reasons why it is at once so far from and so close to myth, and always susceptible to being interpreted a bit mythically.

When Nietzsche says that Christianity is impossible, that it can only lead to absurdities, to outrageous, insane things, it can be said that he's superficially right, even if ultimately he's wrong. You can't get rid of the sacrificial principle by just flicking it away as if it were a piece of dust.

History isn't finished. Every day very interesting things, changes in outlook, are happening right before our eyes. In the United States and everywhere, a lot of current cultural phenomena can be unified by describing them as the discovery of new victims, or rather as their concrete rehabilitation, for in truth we've known about them for a long time: women, children, the elderly, the insane, the physically and mentally handicapped, and so forth. For example, the question of abortion, which has great importance in American debates, is no longer formulated except in the following terms: "Who is the real victim? Is it the child or is it the mother?" You can no longer defend a given position, or indeed any of them, except by making it into a contribution to the anti-victimary crusade.

MT: Do you think that's a good thing or a regression?

RG: In and of itself, it's a good thing. Christian vocabulary and the Christian point of view are insinuating themselves everywhere and becoming universal: it's a sign of the changing times, a sign that Revelation is making progress.

But it is also true that, in many cases, caricatures are taking root, pathological exploitations and hijackings of the victimary obsession. *It's now no longer possible to persecute except in the name of victims!* Once again, Nietzsche saw this already at a time when it was less cartoonish than today: but he didn't see the truth behind the lie.

Just take a look at the reign of terror that's currently being imposed on literature and the social sciences, in other words on the most vulnerable areas of the American university, by the coalition of what's known over there as "single-issue lobbies," ethnic, feminist, neo-Marxist, gay and lesbian pressure groups, and so forth. As soon as concern for victims is universalized in the abstract and becomes an absolute imperative, it can itself become an instrument of injustice. By a sort of overcompensation, there now exists a tendency to make the mere fact of belonging to a minority group a sort of privilege, ensuring the right to tenure, for example, in academia. Each time purely ethnic and social criteria of selection are substituted for pedagogical talent, for the quality of publications, the American university loses what made it so effective, namely merit-based competition. It's transforming itself into a veritable bureaucracy, a system that's hierarchized according to criteria foreign to successful research or even to effective transmission of knowledge. The fact that this hierarchy inverts the former one doesn't constitute progress. From society's vantage point, an upside-down Nietzsche is no better than the right-side-up one who calls for the annihilation of weaklings and losers.

In its extreme forms, the omnipotence of the victim in our world is becoming such that we may be slipping toward the brink of a new totalitarianism.

MT: Well, Christ didn't see that one coming, did he!

RG: Yes he did. The Christian texts predict it. The Gospel of Luke says: "But when the Son of man comes will he find any faith on earth?" The whole Book of Revelation warns of nothing else. What does *Antichrist* mean? It means that we're going to imitate Christ in a parodic way. It's an accurate description of a world—our own—in which the worst acts of persecution are carried out in the name of the fight against persecution. Soviet ideology was nothing else.

One can either explicitly oppose the Christian attitude like the Nazis, or else usurp that attitude and turn it away from its goal, and that's our own brand of totalitarianism. The Nazis said: "We're going to change the West's vocation, we're going to nullify the ideal of a world without victims. We're going to make so many victims that we'll reinstate paganism." Today, on the other hand, the threat in America is the opposite: political correctness.

MT: How do you define political correctness in your vocabulary?

RG: It's the religion of the victim detached from any form of transcendence, the social obligation to employ what amounts to "victimary b.s.," which comes from Christianity but subverts it even more insidiously than open opposition.

MT: Just for laughs, can you give us some choice examples of the latest jargon?

RG: A nice example is the way feminist professors, instead of using the term "seminar," which is seen as too sexist—it comes from *seminarium* ("seed plot"), which is itself derived from *semen*—use the word . . . ovarium!

MT: No . . .

RG: Yes! There's also the "sexual code," officially adopted by Antioch College, in Ohio, which requires males to give a verbal warning to their partner before embarking on any sort of amorous maneuver: "May I place my hand here? May I move my hand in a rhythmic fashion?"

MT: It's Molière's *Learned Ladies* all over again. But, all the same, nobody's about to set up concentration camps or gulags in the name of "political correctness," are they?

RG: Well, there are smarter ways of getting rid of people than the gulag. Maybe we're going to see that.

MT: Every era has its show trials and its witch hunts.

RG: Why, in all witch hunts, in the Stalinist trials, for example, is the victim's confession so important? Because it restores unanimity. When there is true social transcendence, like in a divine right monarchy or in a consensus-driven democracy founded on universal principles, society's unity is not periodically put into question by the death of its representative. "The king is dead, long live the king!" But in a world where the truth stems from a jeopardized unanimity, if the unity cracks it has to be repaired by expelling victims. That's what makes these systems so tragic.

MT: But what convinces the victim to *admit* to being guilty, unlike Job?

RG: Mimetic pressure. Witches always confess, as do those accused of political crimes, as a result of the closure of representation that we were talking about. Human beings live within certain social forms. When they see that everyone is against them, where are they going to find the strength not to confess, on what will they base their refusal? Witches are the doubles of their judges, they share their belief in their own guilt.

MT: So you think for example that, in a Stalinist trial, the accused ended up thinking that he was willing to die if that meant the society would achieve reconciliation?

RG: Not always, but it probably happened. And then, there's the immense prestige of violence. Isn't it true that the prestige of Stalinism decreased (notably among Western intellectuals!) as soon as its degree of violence diminished, as soon as it started to be a little self-critical?

MT: So, where is the limit between the just condemnation of persecutors and the absurd exaggeration of the same phenomenon?

RG: One can't make up rules or provide recipes. The limit lies in the difference between genuine love and pure mimetic resentment. It should never be forgotten that in stable systems the persecutors don't realize that they're persecutors; they don't recognize themselves in the portrait that their victims paint of them when they start to complain. For example, take your average Italian male or even a Frenchman, and tell them that they've always oppressed their wives. At first, they won't believe you. If you force them to, if you keep rubbing their nose in the same realities, over and over, even if they don't admit it, they'll end up glimpsing the truth. And so they'll start criticizing not their own behavior, that would be too much to ask, but the behavior of . . . their ancestors! They'll no doubt end up changing a little bit all the same. When the truth is spoken and repeated, once it finds its way into the public domain, it always ends up making headway. Much faster than seemed possible, a consensus is formed on positions that, just a few years before, still seemed revolutionary and completely inadmissible to conservatives.

There are a lot of abuses in what's been happening in our societies for the last quarter century, but there's also a lot of justice and progress. It's very difficult to keep these two truths in mind at once and to grant each of them the place it deserves. Unfortunately, human beings are made in such a way that righting an injustice always entails the risk of going to the opposite extreme. The mimetic nature of groups makes it that way. Modern societies are like enormous semi-liquid masses that are always in motion. To change their direction even just a little requires unprecedented efforts and extraordinary luck. As soon as success is achieved, the mimetic avalanche threatens to carry off everything in its path. In our era, mimetic desire is reinforced by instantaneous communication and the sensationalism of the media. Whence the importance of politics, and almost invariably its tremendous cowardice, its tendency to go with the flow, like Pilate, in order to get elected, out of an incapacity for independent thought. Above all, one mustn't get stuck in a priori "revolutionary" or "traditional" positions. You see how moderate I am. People think I'm some kind of wild monster because I don't have any Rousseauist illusions about the natural goodness of man, but nothing teaches moderation like the theory of original sin, which is always the opposite of what its critics say it is. Because it always meets with disappointment in reality, the belief in man's natural goodness always leads to the hunt for scapegoats. Indeed, on this point, the story of Rousseau himself and his descent into paranoia are quite exemplary.

CHAPTER 6

A Return to Imitation

MT: Let's go back over the imitation that Plato saw everywhere, except where its role was most important: in acquisitive behaviors, in the competition of desires.

RG: *Mimesis* is the Greek word for imitation. Dance is the most mimetic of all the arts, and indeed it's easy to see its relationship with contagion, the collective trance; we know of its role in sacrifices. In the Gospels themselves, the dance of Salome is a sort of "Rite of Spring" that ends with the prophet's death.

MT: Mimetic desire can only produce evil?

RG: No, it can become bad if it stirs up rivalries but it isn't bad in itself, in fact it's very good, and, fortunately, people can no more give it up than they can give up food or sleep. It is to imitation that we owe not only our traditions, without which we would be helpless, but also, paradoxically, all the innovations about which so much is made today. Modern technology and science show this admirably. Study the history of the world economy and you'll see that since the nineteenth century all the countries that, at a given moment, seemed destined never to play anything but a subordinate role, for lack of "creativity," because of their imitative or, as Montaigne would have said, their "apish" nature, always turned out later on to be more creative than their models.

It began with Germany, which, in the nineteenth century, was thought to be at most capable of imitating the English, and this at the precise moment it surpassed them. It continued with the Americans in whom, for a long time, the Europeans saw mediocre gadget-makers who weren't theoretical or cerebral enough to take on a world leadership role. And it happened once more with the Japanese who, after World War II, were still seen as pathetic imitators of Western superiority. It's starting up again, it seems, with Korea, and soon, perhaps, it'll be the Chinese.

All of these consecutive mistakes about the creative potential of imitation cannot be due to chance. To make an effective imitator, you have to openly admire the model you're imitating, you have to acknowledge your imitation. You have to explicitly recognize the superiority of those who succeed better than you and set about learning from them.

If a businessman sees his competitor making money while he's losing money, he doesn't have time to reinvent his whole production process. He imitates his more fortunate rivals.

In business, imitation remains possible today because mimetic vanity is less involved than in the arts, in literature, and in philosophy. In the most spiritual domains, the modern world rejects imitation in favor of originality at all costs. You should never say what others are saying, never paint what others are painting, never think what others are thinking, and so on. Since this is absolutely impossible, there soon emerges a negative imitation that sterilizes everything. Mimetic rivalry cannot flare up without becoming destructive in a great many ways.

We can see it today in the so-called soft sciences (which fully deserve the name). More and more often they're obliged to turn their coats inside out and, with great fanfare, announce some new "epistemological rupture" that is supposed to revolutionize the field from top to bottom.

This rage for originality has produced a few rare masterpieces and quite a few rather bizarre things in the style of Jacques Lacan's *Écrits*. Just a few years ago the mimetic escalation had become so insane that it drove everyone to make himself more incomprehensible than his peers. In American universities the imitation of those models has since produced some pretty comical results. But today that lemon has been squeezed completely dry. The principle of originality at all costs leads to paralysis. The more we celebrate "creative and enriching" innovations, the fewer of them there are. So-called postmodernism is even more sterile than modernism, and, as its name suggests, also totally dependent on it.

For two thousand years the arts have been imitative, and it's only in the nineteenth and twentieth centuries that people started refusing to be mimetic. Why? Because we're more mimetic than ever. Rivalry plays a role such that we strive vainly to exorcise imitation.

MT: Indeed, up until Molière, Racine, and Marivaux, authors constantly looked back to their predecessors to find themes for their works.

RG: Starting with the Quarrel of the Ancients and the Moderns at the end of the seventeenth century, people began to wonder whether the superiority of the Ancients hadn't been usurped, but they imitated anyway. It was only with the symbolists, at the end of the nineteenth century, that imitation was forbidden, that it was turned into a scapegoat in all areas of intellectual and cultural life, even in psychology.

In my opinion, the new can only emerge within a tradition. You can't subvert tradition except from within. Once you are exterior to everything, you're in the void and there you stay. That's where I think we are today. The more we condemn imitation, the more we surrender to it under various guises. Fashion has never been more powerful than it is today. Intellectual life is nothing more than a series of frantic infatuations, until the system starts to break down.

MT: All the same, there are also bad uses of tradition, bad uses of the kind of respect that leads to confinement. The professors who are content to be collectors of philosophical history, the ones who are just admirers or even just critics of their predecessors, will never be true philosophers themselves, true inventors of philosophies. You're well aware of this since, though you may want to recall certain forgotten truths, with an original thinker like you, despite what you may say, there's the desire to start with a clean slate, to "live on the edge" as a thinker.

RG: There are models who should be forgotten and others who must be respected or rediscovered, and there's no way to tell in advance which is which. But human beings are essentially mimetic, saintliness is mimetic, innovation is mimetic, breakthroughs are always mimetic. Repetition and boredom are too.

MT: But the new, the absolutely new? The world is being transformed, science comes up with new inventions every day, and it's also true that Kandinsky's "First Abstract Watercolor" was indeed the first; nobody had painted like that before, it really was new. Even if one thinks, as you do, that "the new can only emerge within a tradition," for innovation to appear mustn't one stop imitating at some point?

RG: If the absolutely new exists, it cannot be codified. Often that which is relatively new is born of the unexpected encounter between two objects or two levels of reality that seemed unlikely to come together. And, once more, it's ritual that brings the encounter about, because, as you recall, it stages crisis. It is therefore perfectly capable of generating incongruous mixtures, but in a regulated and methodical way, and not in the vertiginous spirit that accompanies real mimetic crisis. Ritual is a creative crisis because it is partially simulated and always a little bit under control. Thus it isn't contradictory to celebrate both tradition and innovation.

I think that's the meaning of the sacrifice of Isaac, which marks the abandonment of human sacrifice, the shift to animal sacrifice. What's extraordinary about this Biblical text is that it first shows us an Abraham who is still obedient to the system of human sacrifice. It shows the obedience first: it shows that it's out of that obedience that true change becomes possible.

I think the destruction of forms has a history. It's an aesthetic, and it lasts for a hundred or so years at most. But the construction of forms is not just something aesthetic, and it is much more important than their destruction. Even in the aesthetic domain, it's clear that our civilization is unlike any other. It was only the Christian West that discovered perspective and the photographic realism that we're always badmouthing: it was also the Christian West that invented cameras. No other culture ever invented them. A researcher who works in this field once remarked to me that, in Western trompe l'oeil, every object is deformed according to the same principles with respect to light and space: it's the pictorial equivalent of God letting the sun shine and the rain fall on the just and the unjust. No longer are the socially important people portrayed as big and the others as little. There is an absolute equality of perception. The current aesthetic keeps trying to hide from itself the importance of our uniqueness, but the attempt won't last forever. It's in the process of collapsing.

MT: That's Régis Debray's thesis: the incarnation of Christ and the defeat of the iconoclasts gave the West mastery of images and thus of innovation. Here's a question that may be absurd: does a phrase like "if someone hits you on one cheek, turn the other" have anything to do with imitation?

RG: Of course it does, since it's directed against "adversarial" imitation, and is one and the same thing as the imitation of Christ. In the Gospels, everything is imitation, since Christ himself seeks to imitate and be imitated. Unlike the modern gurus who claim to be imitating nobody, but who want to be imitated on that basis, Christ says: "Imitate me as I imitate the Father."

The rules of the Kingdom of God are not at all utopian: *if you want to put an end to mimetic rivalry, give way completely to your rival.* You nip rivalry in the bud. We're not talking about a political program, this is a lot simpler and more fundamental. If someone is making excessive demands on you, he's already involved in mimetic rivalry, he expects you to participate in the escalation. So, to put a stop to it, the only means is to do the opposite of what escalation calls for: meet the excessive demand twice over. If you've been told to walk a mile, walk two; if you've been hit on the left cheek, offer up the right. The Kingdom of God is nothing but this, but that doesn't mean it's easily accessible.

There is also a pretty strong unwritten tradition that states that "Satan is the ape of God." Satan is extremely paradoxical in the Gospels. First he is mimetic disorder, but he is also order because he is the *prince of this world.* When the Pharisees accuse him of freeing the possessed from their demons by the power of "Beelzebub," Jesus replies: "Now if Satan drives out Satan, he is divided against himself; so how can his kingdom last? [. . .] But if it is through the Spirit of God that I drive out devils, then be sure that the kingdom of God has caught you unawares." This means that Satan's order is the order of the scapegoat. Satan is the whole mimetic system in the Gospels.

That Satan is temptation, that Satan is rivalry that turns against itself—all the traditions see this; succumbing to temptation always means tempting others. What the Gospel adds, and what is unique to it, I think, is that *Satan is order.* The order of this world is not divine, it's sacrificial, it's satanic in a certain sense. That doesn't mean that religions are satanic, it means that the mimetic system, in its eternal return, enslaves humanity. Satan's transcendence is precisely that violence temporarily masters itself in the scapegoat phenomenon: Satan never expels himself once and for all—only the Spirit of God can do that—but he more or less "chains himself" by means of the sacrificial order. All medieval legends tell you: *the devil asks for but one victim,* but as for that victim, he can't do without it. If you don't obey the rules of the Kingdom of God, you are necessarily dependent on Satan.

Satan means "the Accuser." And the Spirit of God is called *Paraclete,* that is to say "the Defender of Victims," it's all there. The defender of victims reveals the inanity of Satan by showing that his accusations are untruthful. Oedipus's parricide and incest, which give the plague to a whole community—they're a joke, a very bad joke that helps cause quite a bit of damage among us when we take it seriously, as, in the final analysis, is the case with . . . the psychoanalysts: they take the lie of the Accuser seriously. Our whole culture is dominated by mythical accusation to the extent that it does not denounce it. Psychoanalysis endorses the accusation.

CHAPTER 7

Science

MT: The consensus is that Christianity has never ceased to lag behind on the question of scientific development, to oppose the new worldviews attached to theories of physics such as Galileo's. But in truth, you say, at a deeper level, it is really Christianity that makes science possible by *desacralizing* the real, by freeing people from magical causalities. Once we stop seeing storms as being triggered by the machinations of the witch across the street, we start being able to study meteorological phenomena scientifically.

Once again, current events seem to confirm your thesis. The Soviet Union was built on an ode to scientific progress, it enjoyed a few notable successes, was able, at first, to build up its heavy industry and to send the first man into space. Even the partisans of liberal democracy were hardly optimistic until the 1960s: it seemed that respecting human rights hindered the efficiency of the countries that adopted them, and that they would never be able to fight on equal terms with the unscrupulous dictatorships that had the manpower of their subjects at their disposal. And then, surprisingly, the religion of Moloch collapsed and exposed its rusty joints: Chernobyl, the dried-up Aral Sea, an obsolete industrial infrastructure ... what a grisly end! In his book, Fukuyama relates one Soviet citizen's observation that, at the same time as he was promised that he would be "eating pineapple on the moon," he still couldn't "find his fill of tomatoes on earth"![1] The sky was no longer the limit for the materialists. It was as if things, at the same time as people, had decided not to be Marxist anymore. It would thus seem that "recognizing victims' rights" is also a better management principle than ruling with an iron fist.

RG: Very true.

MT: How would you describe the origin of technologies and the relationship between Christianity and science?

RG: In the first sacrificial societies, ritual provided a model of action and cultures applied this model in the most varied situations, with various outcomes. For example, when people dance around to make springtime come, we say: "There you have religion—how absurd! Springtime doesn't need anyone to make it come." But when these same people extract iron ore, melt it down, and say that they're accelerating sacred processes, we recognize the beginnings of metallurgy. On the other hand, if they do more or less the same thing with gold, indicating that they're seeking a form of perfection, we say once again that it's superstition and alchemy. In my opinion, there is no initial difference among these various attitudes: there are cultures that get lucky and others that don't.

MT: Technologies are born haphazardly, through experimentation, and are either confirmed or not by reality. Isn't this a very Darwinian point of view?

RG: To tell you the truth, I don't know. But I think that Darwin and his whole era failed to see the creative power of ritual. As I was saying earlier, and contrary to what its apparent monotony and repetitiveness might lead us to think, ritual is creative in the cultural realm because it involves disorder that's a little orderly or order that's a little disorderly. Ritual gives birth to techniques because it makes it possible to mix things that taboos keep apart. And that's how new things come about, that's what we call experimentation.

MT: But Christianity destroys ritual?

RG: That's true, but starting in an era when archaic rites have lost their fecundity, when we no longer need them. By desacralizing the world, Christianity has given us the means of transforming into a readily-available technique the creative imitation that ritual can probably produce only once, when it still has the energy that later disappears through repetition.

MT: And yet many non-Christian civilizations distinguished themselves in the early ages of science: the Greeks, the Arabs, the Jews, even the Mayans. Thales, for example, supposedly already had the idea that phenomena were due not to the caprices of Zeus but to natural laws. In other words, doesn't the invention of science—and I'm actually talking about science this time, about abstract mathematics, and not technologies—come out of the pagan world?

RG: In the ancient world, only a few individually emancipated intellectuals or the religious castes practiced the kind of observation that leads to science. It was a leisure activity reserved for a miniscule elite. The intellectual and spiritual freedom that it requires is the result of a favorable coincidence between an individual's natural talents and his birth in a milieu that was sufficiently privileged to ensure that they would blossom.

From the fifteenth century, democratization is a fundamental given, inseparable from the importance in our world of technological applications that, as is quite obvious, the aristocratic science of antiquity took hardly any interest in. Heidegger thinks that in our world technology always precedes and "drives" science. His thesis seems too one-sided to me.

MT: And yet that's what you just said yourself when you described technologies as emerging haphazardly from ritual.

RG: But Heidegger speaks only of modern science. His "Schritt zurück," his "step back," stops with the pre-Socratics: what he fails to see is precisely that technology is rooted in ritual. On the other hand, what seems true to me is that the more science develops, the more the mutually exclusive realms of technology and science tend to bleed into each other. It's possible that ancient science came to a standstill because its indifference to technical applications fated it to die of hunger. The idea of a resolutely experimental science seems to me democratic in its very principle. It is now understood that experimentation is a part of "pure" science, but why did this principle gain traction so belatedly? In an aristocratic universe, experimentation smacks of impurity and the rabble, precisely because it forces researchers to "get their hands dirty"—that's something aristocrats never do voluntarily, they have servants to spare them the unpleasantness. But that's also their loss: if, as in Aristotle's republic, you have enough slaves to push the chariots or even to haul you around like donkeys, why go to great lengths to invent the internal combustion engine?

Only experimentation reveals the true domain of the so-called hard sciences, the domain where mathematical applications are possible. This domain doesn't overlap with the objectifiable in the sense of the subject-object opposition, but with the non-human, with all fields where human freedom isn't there to undermine mathematical calculation. The possibility for science in the experimental sense exists wherever human interference can be more or less neutralized, or made constant enough so that it's still possible to make predictions—which quite often hold true only on the statistical level.

The successes of science have given rise to an enormous amount of idolatry and have led to its being considered as a group of specific methods: but its success, it seems to me, is due less to method than to the type of object studied by thinking freed from the ancient constraints of the sacred. This success is so intoxicating that the social and human sciences never give up hoping to become "truly scientific" by transporting the methods that work in the hard sciences into their domains. All they end up doing is impoverishing their own objects of study.

If the object cannot be adapted to the method, the method must be adapted to the object. That's what mimetic theory strives to do. Far from being naively reductive and deterministic, as people sometimes say, it shows that in human affairs the unpredictable is always possible. The sequences that it uncovers are very probable because they are the automatic reflexes of sin, but they are never certain. There is never any determinism in the strong sense of the word.

MT: Modern physicists argue a lot about the notion of "reality," which they fail to define. Bohr thought that it was meaningless and that we could speak only of perceptions and empirical measure-results. Whereas Einstein, to the contrary, was absolutely convinced that there was a real world that existed independently of our senses, a world that it was precisely science's mission to describe. In your view, the real world exists independently of us and of our senses, and you even put your trust in common sense.

RG: That's right. That said, I find it admirable that we spend fortunes building ever more immense particle accelerators and even launching telescopes into space. And yet I fear that we'll never find anything but the next generation of particles; and that we'll then have to build a new cyclotron as big as the entire Earth, and then we'll find another generation of particles, and so on.

MT: Note that if we reach the limits of the Earth, we'll be obliged to stop ... Space has its limits, its "finitude," as they say. We're prisoners of this little sphere.

RG: We're not going to make contact with absolute reality, we're going to continue to discover new worlds. But that doesn't prevent me from being on Einstein's side rather than Bohr's. If I go out, I'm going to find the corner bakery, which was there yesterday and will be there tomorrow. I can't help thinking that this certainty and regularity of our perceptions reveals a fundamental dimension of the real, of created being. This realism is implied in all of my work.

MT: The loss of contact with reality is the simplest way of defining madness. There is something disturbing about science and knowledge playing this dangerous game.

A brief digression: I don't know if you're familiar with the mad and delicious detective stories of the eccentric (and Catholic) English writer—greatly prized by Jorge Luis Borges, to whom I owe my discovery of him—Gilbert Keith Chesterton. His favorite detectives are a young poet with his head in the clouds and a little chubby curate, Father Brown, whose activities are generally inspired by a philosophy similar to yours, by the desire to free people from false causalities. In one of the stories, the poet-detective notices a young man who is behaving strangely and diagnoses the imminent onset of madness because, a sudden rainstorm having on two occasions coincided with his presence at two consecutive garden parties, the idea that he may well be a sort of rain god with the power to unleash storms gradually takes possession of him! Our extraordinary bloodhound-cum-psychiatrist saves the unfortunate fellow and leads him back to reason . . . by tying him to a tree naked on a stormy night to demonstrate to him that he can't command the elements. To give an idea of the story's intriguing charm, I must add that it is constructed backwards: you begin by seeing a sort of maniacal crazy person tying a miserable victim to a tree, in a maelstrom of water and lightning. But the truth is revealed to be at odds with appearances.

RG: I've never read the Father Brown stories. I'm familiar only with Chesterton's admirable essays. I've never heard them mentioned in France: he's the most vibrant modern apologist of Christianity.

The only allowable conversion these days has to do . . . with science. We're asked to believe that the Scientific Spirit descended on mankind like some kind of Revelation. I'm not kidding. That's what the schoolbooks say. Children are taught that we stopped hunting witches because of the advent of science. When in fact it's the opposite: science took hold because, for moral and religious reasons, we stopped hunting witches.

A certain brand of contemporary feminism would like to rehabilitate witches and pretend that they were really witches. In my opinion, it's a very poor tactic. Witchcraft doesn't exist, that's where we should start, you're thought to be a witch only because of a system of accusation. That said, some women no doubt felt that the accusation of witchcraft made them unique . . . so that they even wanted to be witches: that would be the grain of truth in Michelet's thesis. That didn't prevent them from being mistaken, from wasting their time on unspeakable foolishness.

MT: I still don't think that you can say that the accusation always comes first, that it creates witchcraft, which wouldn't exist otherwise. Even leaving aside the question of whether magical knowledge has meaning, it seems to me that there were at least some people who believed in it, no?

RG: Of course. There really were people who danced around cauldrons of frogs and scorpions, but we *know* today that their spells and chanting wouldn't keep airplanes from flying. That's why terrorists prefer bombs to witchcraft. That's why, even when they were condemned, even when they were technically guilty, witches were scapegoats.

MT: It's very paradoxical. Not only do you judge other civilizations, but now you're also judging others eras from the "omega point" of your certitude.

RG: Are you such a devout cultural relativist that you believe that, at least in some cultures, witchcraft is true and that it has objective effects that aren't just mimetic?

MT: Getting back to those same pagan Greeks whose role in developing science we were examining, they're also credited with simultaneously inventing democracy. I'm well aware of the limits of its initial form, which concerned only a small community of male citizens and excluded everyone else—the "Barbarians," slaves, women—and didn't know any sort of Christian-like universalism. But, all the same, do think that we should make room alongside the Judeo-Christian heritage for the Greek heritage?

RG: You must be joking. Make room for the Greeks in our culture? Why, we've been doing little else since the thirteenth century and even before. In our intellectual history there are periods where Plato is dominant and others where it's Aristotle. And it was the Church that first set the tone. Not for nothing did it invent the university, for which it is always a matter of reconciling Revelation with Greek philosophy—Plato and Aristotle—even if that meant that eventually there'd be no more Revelation, just the Greeks. The first academic, Abelard, was as Greek as you could be in his era, and mimetic as hell given that he invented academic rivalry and erotic teacher-student relationships.

All our Renaissances and humanisms are nothing but returns to the Greeks. The Revolution and the Empire are both obsessed with the Greeks. And the most influential modern thinkers—Nietzsche, Heidegger, and a few others—also swear only by the Greeks. True, every era tends to reject the Greeks that were most prized by the preceding era, but always in the name of other Greeks, and as a general rule, ever more ancient Greeks, whose archaism makes them seem even more Greek than the newer ones. We're in search of ever more intoxicating Hellenic elixirs. Asking our culture to make room for the Greeks is like asking Los Angeles to make room for the automobile. I have no desire to eliminate the Greeks, and I talk about them a lot—but why can't we talk a little about something else now and then?

Fundamentally, we're always trying to minimize or brush aside the Judaic and the Christian in official culture, in the university. If you talk about Christianity without beating it the way one beats a dead horse, you risk seeing the walls of a ghetto rise up around you, a ghetto that, let it be said in passing, is even more closed off in the United States than it is in France.

As far as the invention of democracy is concerned, I disagree with you there, too. A democracy that excludes foreigners, women, and slaves, and that is based entirely on the exploitation of a colonial or semi-colonial empire is worth no more than lots of other oligarchies. I have intense admiration for Greek culture, but for me Greece already represents everything that in Western culture is seen as being most blameworthy: rabid nationalism, colonialism, sexism, racism, and so forth. I don't see why everything that is very abominable in us would be very admirable in the Greeks.

CHAPTER 8

The One and the Many

MT: Is the uniformization of the world a mandatory ransom for progress, material progress on the one hand and progress of conscience and solidarity on the other? Are we heading toward a single civilization?

RG: I think so. The closure of societies is linked to "scapegoat" type practices. To close is always to define an outside and an inside by means of exclusions and expulsions. As a result, the more these practices weaken, the more exteriority loses ground. Insofar as there are no more victims to close society, it's opening up; and we're heading more and more toward a mono-culture.

MT: Just a little more theory before coming back to more concrete aspects. I have some difficulty in locating the stages of differentiation and uniformization in the process described by your hypothesis. We start originally from an indistinct crowd that splits up into particular cultures—and in the end we come back to a homogeneous whole through the destruction of those cultures, which were also systems that oppressed individuals.

RG: Yes, but at the beginning, without the ravages of violent mimetic rivalries, there wouldn't have been differentiations that engendered oppositions, there would have been no mutually excluding systems of representation. There would have flourished only forms of diversity that we have trouble imagining today. So instead of seeing a single process of differentiation, we should imagine a multitude of processes that don't necessarily depend on one another.

With Christianity, we're of course dealing with something else: there really is at work among us a tendency toward global undifferentiation and toward a certain unification of the planet. Which doesn't necessarily mean an end to all variety: the Christian Middle Ages created diversity in unity, whether you're talking about languages or architectural styles; a Romanesque church in Poitou doesn't look like a Romanesque church in Provence, and so forth. Europe was one, and it was only because of nationalism that this global harmony was later destroyed.

MT: I don't know if you can really say that the Christian Middle Ages were a source of diversity: instead, it seems to me that they didn't entirely succeed in destroying the diversity that they inherited from pre-Christian times.

RG: Most of the diversity whose erasure you deplore comes from the Middle Ages.

MT: To come back to the present day and the future, do you mean to say that, within the unified civilization that would be the outcome of human evolution after Revelation, we might be able to rediscover unsuspected forms of diversity? That we might be able to replace the differences between civilizations with differences between groups, generations, and so on?

RG: Yes, diversity in unity . . . diversity of a kind unseen since the old world.

MT: This uniformization is not a surprise. It is explicitly heralded in the founding texts of Christianity. Saint Paul—who recommended to the Jews that they abandon the Mosaic Law, which is to say their rites, which is to say their culture—was already saying in his letters that, in the Kingdom of Christ, "There can be neither Jew nor Greek, there can be neither slave nor freeman," but that everyone is "all one in Christ Jesus."

RG: In fact, you'll find the same idea expressed in the Hebrew Bible four or five hundred years earlier, in the Old Testament, on the lips of the prophet Joel, one of the "minor prophets" who is the "prophet of the Spirit," who foretells that on the chosen day "even on the slaves, men and women, shall I pour out my spirit." This is very close to Paul, who by the way didn't recommend to the Jews that they abandon the Law. He said that the *gentiles* who became Christian could not be required to observe the law. That's not the same thing.

What you say about abandoning rites must be nuanced. One of the principal texts would be:

> So then, if you are bringing your offering to the altar and there remember that your brother has something against you, leave your offering there before the altar, go and be reconciled with your brother first, and then come back and present your offering. (Matthew 5:23–24)

This isn't entirely anti-ritual, but ritual is rejected in a secondary way. The prophets are sometimes more radical. Christ repeats what one of them says: "For faithful love is what pleases me, not sacrifice." The Church knows very well that ritual is first and foremost social: thus the Church is in charge of certain prescriptions and can also do away with them, like "Fish on Friday," and so forth. In my opinion, Paul reads the Gospels very correctly when he says that "everything is permitted" if there is love, but that "not everything is recommended." You mustn't scandalize your brothers. For example, it's better not to eat sacrificial meat when you're in the company of people for whom that would be wrong. The end of all "laws" in the rigid, non-adaptable sense is still at the foundation of Christianity, but the main idea is that, if you truly love, you'll go above and beyond the Law. "Turn the other cheek" is a good example of this "above and beyond."

Christianity speaks unceasingly of the "powers of this world," which are the institutions born of the sacrificial system. It says that they must be respected to the extent that they don't ask anything that's contrary to faith, but it adds that they're destined to fade away because of the corroding effects of Revelation. The Powers and Principalities are always presented as united against Christ: in my opinion this isn't some historical indication, it's a definition. These institutions are based on the victimary mechanism. The theory of the Powers and Principalities is part of the revelation of the earthly order and the violence that constitutes it.

MT: By taking this "anti-ritualism" to extremes, doesn't Revelation also herald the end of the Church itself?

RG: It's true that the texts of Christianity refer to the possibility of its failure in this world. "The time is sure to come when people will not accept sound teaching, but their ears will be itching for anything new and they will collect themselves a whole series of teachers according to their own tastes; and then they will shut their ears to the truth and will turn to myths." If someone had told French people of the seventeenth century, Jansenists, Jesuits, or what have you, that Christianity would be where it is now, with empty churches everywhere and a good portion of the clergy no longer believing in anything but sociology and psychoanalysis, they obviously would have been wide-eyed with astonishment.

And yet, although many so-called progressive Christians see the demise of the Church as the fulfillment of Christianity, in truth the Gospels don't predict anything of the kind and to the contrary say that "the gates of the underworld can never overpower the Church" (Matthew 16:18).

Granted, Christian culture as it has existed until now is ailing. The modern process that is destroying cultures is also destroying the one culture that is historically the most central, the one that predicted and initiated the process. All of the various European nations in succession have played a role in "globalization": it began with the Italians in the thirteenth and fourteenth centuries; then the Spanish, the Portuguese, the French, the English, the Germans, and the Americans. Tomorrow, maybe it will be the Japanese. It's not quite clear how Christian they are, obviously . . . [*laughter*] . . . but they're operating all the same within the one global system.

You speak of cultural variety: do you really think that variety still exists? Of course human groups and religions still share the world, there are borders, but fundamentally what separates them anymore, what differentiates us from the Islamic countries? Economic possibilities, educational methods? Cultures are already unified in most of the concepts they use, in their communication systems, their consumer goods. We now have a planetary language: English.

MT: Now wait just a minute. There's more than a small difference between undergoing uniformization and welcoming it. Had the prophet Joel done nothing but announce the unification of mankind, undifferentiation would probably have occurred anyway under the impact of slow changes that might well have been peaceful and voluntary. But Paul's letters look more like a program for *organizing* mankind's homogenization, rallying us to the cause. This, in any event, is how the Church understood them historically, sending out missionaries alongside soldiers and merchants. Today, it has changed its tune, and wishes to project a more tolerant image: but, if I understand you correctly, this might well be because there's now no harm in doing so, because the essential aspect of the cultures in question has already been destroyed. Why hasn't Christianity been similarly profitable to the other peoples (I'm thinking mostly of Africans and South American Indians) that we have Christianized? Doesn't that show that the right explanation for our success is not Christianity but rather the colonial violence that we've exercised and that we continue to exercise against these peoples?

RG: The one doesn't necessarily exclude the other. Christianity never says that it's going to do away with sin. God created free beings capable of evil (colonial violence) as well as good (the protection of victims). Christianity says only that a global Revelation is at work in the world, the effects of which may be either beneficial or negative, as a result not of sacred caprice but of the use to which we put our freedom. All we can do is note what happens, what human freedom makes of the possibilities it is offered.

MT: But then that means that Christianity, far from having set forth an original position, was merely the instrument for something inevitable. It's the messenger of God, or else of the Devil, depending on what you think about the homogenization of mankind.

RG: There's been a misunderstanding. I have no desire to defend what we're calling the undifferentiation of cultures. I'm even less ready to do so given that, unlike so many others, I don't see it as a source of peace and tranquility. To the contrary, I think that the present conflicts are already rooted in undifferentiation much more than in differences that have become obsolete and are no longer anything but pretexts.

What I'm saying is that, even if the current state of the world isn't reassuring, even if human beings are doing their best to transform the Christian promise into a nightmare, the nostalgia for the archaic and the pagan that our world feels so strongly appears to me to be based on a frightening illusion. Think of the twenty thousand victims that Aztec priests sacrificed every year. Their cities, though they may have been beautiful, were awash in innocent blood. In this five-hundredth anniversary of Columbus's journey, it's considered good form to forget about these horrors; just as we forget that the Europe of that era was not the Europe of today: compared to us, the conquistadors too were primitive. Both were part of a historical process that can only be judged globally. If you declare the Aztecs innocent, then grant the same thing to Columbus. If you're going to judge, condemn the crimes of both camps and acknowledge that the Europeans put an end to unspeakable rituals.

MT: But why wouldn't legal states respecting human rights be enough to fulfill the Christian promise? Why must all peoples be evangelized? What if some people don't want to be Christian, what if they see it as something specific to whites and Westerners that negates their own specificity?

RG: You think exactly like the so-called progressive churches. What I'm talking about no longer depends on individuals' adherence to Christianity. The countries that don't want to be Christian have no problem coming to the UN and telling us: "We are victims! Therefore, you have to do something!"

In doing so, they're speaking an essentially Christian language. They're inserting themselves into a Christianized context.

The destruction of cultural diversity is due less to missionaries and soldiers than it is to the strong attraction exercised by the modern West. Even Islamic fundamentalism, which appears to open up a chasm between the Christian world and the Muslim world, is perhaps only a "dialectical" reaction to the reverse—and considerably deeper—phenomenon, namely Islam's entry into the modern world: besides, fundamentalism isn't anti-technology, it's not anti-modern. It is born of the observation that the modernization of these countries is necessarily an imitation of the West: that's hard to swallow. So, there's the desire to modernize in the name of the value that sets them apart, which is Islam.

The people who, speaking of "the return of religion," cite such phenomena to challenge the idea that the planet is being unified, don't recognize that they are signs of new advances in the fundamental principles that come from Christianity.

The arrogance of the modern West is linked to the demystifying power that it alone possessed for several centuries and whose origin it never bothers to investigate seriously. It's a real superiority, and we shouldn't deny it, as we are striving to do in our era. What must be denied, though, is the idea that this superiority, which is only temporary, is our own creation, and that we owe the enlightenment we enjoy to our exceptional merit. Desacralization, which in fact is of Christian origin, has been accompanied by de-Christianization, by a loss of the *humilitas* of the early Christians, and Westerners have fallen prey to a cultural vanity that they are now more conscious of but from which they're having trouble extracting themselves. For some time, the West took itself for a masterpiece of nature of which it was itself the author. Our era is right to react to this, but it immediately goes to the opposite extreme, as always happens in such cases. For the last thirty years, we've made it our duty to regard ourselves as the most monstrous creatures in all of History. This is no more true than was nineteenth century cultural pride. The common denominator of all these excesses is the desire to minimize and even to condemn the religious and cultural forces to which we owe the relative cultural superiority that we're misusing. It's actually because we're idolaters of this relative superiority that we think we're obliged to deny its existence.

MT: You were talking earlier about "mono-culture." But you're sometimes even more radical and speak of "non-culture" to define the social state that is awaiting us. This is logical if every culture is defined by its system of rites and if all of these systems are falling apart. You say that the reason we can't define this future society is that we are enclosed in our current system of representation. But all the same, the idea of a "non-culture" makes me shudder. We can't speak abstractly about the death of cultures, because they only exist because of human beings. To marginalize a culture doesn't merely mean ceasing to worry about it, printing fewer dictionaries: it means brainwashing its members, for whom it's the only means of accessing the world, or in any event their privileged means of access, the one that defines them; and quite often it means killing them. Just look at the uniformization of our lifestyles, their Americanization as people sometimes say, without seeing that the Americans may be the primary victims of a universal process rather than its masters: can you really say that this is a Christian achievement, an achievement of Love? Isn't it instead the diktat of a leveling logic that reduces us all not to people of the same culture but to registration numbers, subhumans without any culture at all?

RG: What goes by the name of "uniformization," the end of differences, of particular cultures, is always something very ambiguous; it's at once the worst and the best, the covering up of the Christian message, the posturing of the Antichrist, rampant hypocrisy, but also more truth. So we shouldn't speak ill of today's world, nor look to the past with nostalgia. The only possible humanism today consists in pushing our thinking about this coexistence of the worst and the best as far as it can go: then we see that we're caught up in an incredible act of creation that completely surpasses our understanding. We can't clearly see the rhyme and reason of it all, but we can hold out hope that it's not just the death of a civilization. The "mimetic suffering" of someone who earns a decent living and who envies the billionaire next door isn't exactly on the same level as the suffering of people who died of hunger and malnutrition in the Middle Ages. We shouldn't worship technology, but we shouldn't curse it either. Moderation alone is helpful; balance and wisdom.

MT: I'm going to lay out a theory that's different from yours, and you can react to my exposition. You say that it's Christian revelation that triggers this uniformization, for Good. But what if it was instead—for Evil—a sort of man- and culture-eating ogress? An ogress that we could call *Logic*, which quite simply wants homogenous crowds so as to be able to manage them (an eminently modern notion) all at once, by taking just one identical individual into consideration. The ogress would surreptitiously replace all universalist philosophies and religions as soon as they achieved a majority. In this way, socialism and Christianity would be authentically good so long as they represented the hopes of an oppressed minority (the individual's right to revolt against the power of the fathers) but would in turn become brainwashing machines ("culturewashing" machines) as soon as they acquired power. We could find evidence of this process in the "non-art" of modern design and architecture: our buildings, in the shape of cubes and parallelepipeds, aren't the art of any civilization, they're the "non-art" of logic, of the degree zero of necessity (shelter); if you put people in there (Arabs, Portuguese, French people) what comes out is just a bunch of inter-changeable bodies. By the same token, the hamburgers that are taking over the planet aren't the fruit of the culinary techniques of any culture: they're just a dose of calories. Logic has stolen the earth away from mankind. This pessimistic theory doesn't expose itself to the accusation of ethnocentrism that can be leveled at your optimism.

RG: The real problem is that God doesn't have any meaning for you apart from his relationship to society. What I'm trying to tell you is that even the worst things about our society make it possible to glimpse a God who is infinitely transcendent with respect to all of that, but who, in spite of every-thing, takes an interest in us, strives to help us come closer to Him. You can't make Christian revelation responsible for people's misuse of it.

MT: My hypothesis says, on the one hand, that the uniformization of cultures is bad, and a loss, and on the other that, without Christ, we would have wit-nessed the same phenomenon.

RG: No doubt, but then there wouldn't be any hope. I prefer to think that what we're witnessing is the collapse of Satan's system. Before, Satan "leashed himself" by means of the sacrificial order. Thus, the end of Satan, the end of his self-leashing signifies not his disappearance, but literally his "unleashing." Satan always follows Christ. There is a complex relationship between the two of them. To have faith is to think that, in the final analysis, all of this has meaning, it's to have confidence not in History, but in the Absolute. The chief enemy is nihilism, and what you've just said tends toward it.

It's nihilism that we have to fight against if we want to fight for mankind, wouldn't you say?

To remain humanist today, one has to become religious again. If it's true that Malraux said something like "The twenty-first century will be religious or it will not be," it's my interpretation of those words that I'm offering you.

MT: Destroying what was oppressive about a culture is one thing. But a culture is also a language, an art, a worldview: can there be such a thing as an individual without culture?

RG: No, I think not, indeed.

MT: Don't we also need certain rites in order to feel like we belong to a group? Why couldn't there be harmless rites, mere good living habits?

RG: There are such rites. Social rituals are also instruments of love. Matthew shows very clearly that marriage, indissoluble monogamy, represents progress over the repudiation of wives by husbands. You just have to open your eyes to see that nothing has changed. Work habits are ritualistic in a certain sense. Another domain in which "good habits" are indispensable is creation. Civilization and culture are impossible without controlled repetition. That's why Trotsky's idea of a "permanent revolution" is not only the height of metaphysical revolt, but also an immense stupidity. All creators know this.

MT: The local "habits" you're talking about have colored Christianity itself, and today's Church doesn't shy away from talking here and there of "cultural integration." Historically speaking, the fusion between Christianity and local cultures sometimes happened all by itself. And it's most interesting when it's the local culture that fuses with Christianity instead of the other way around. For example, it's been noted how extremely easy it was for the Druidic West to welcome the Christian message: it's as if they were waiting for it, as if these peoples had themselves made strides toward the same universal values. There wasn't a single Christian martyr in those lands, and Irish monks were the ones who finally saw to the European continent's conversion to Christianity. And this to such a degree that, but for the involvement of the Celtic world, Christianity might well have remained nothing but a Jewish heresy.

RG: Where the successful or failed dialogues between Christianity and other cultures are concerned, we could go on for hours. We could recall the sixteenth century in Japan, where the number of Christians had reached one hundred thousand before the imperial power decided to close off the country against this threat. In one of Kurosawa's movies you see missionaries blessing the warriors who are going off to battle. And in the eighteenth century, too, the Jesuit missionaries who had gone to China and developed close ties with the emperor returned to the pope with the following message: "The emperor is ready to convert, and all his people with him, if we allow them to maintain the ancestor worship cult." It's one of the most prodigious moments in the history of the world.

MT: So what happened? Judging by the result, it must not have worked.

RG: The pope concluded that it went against Christianity, and they were told no.

MT: Do you think that pope was right?

RG: I don't know.

MT: I'd like to emphasize one of the most troubling aspects of your theory and of the Christian texts, one that we already mentioned during our first overview at the beginning of these conversations: Revelation doesn't say anything about the future toward which it's propelling us.

RG: Christ explicitly says that "as for that day and hour, nobody knows it, neither the angels of heaven, nor the Son, no one but the Father alone."

And yet, when faced with people who are telling us that "we're just random fragments of matter" or that we're caught up "in a history that doesn't have any meaning," we can reply: "No, look at what's happening, look at what's growing bigger every day, look what came out of this Text like a genie from a bottle." It's not a matter of predicting the future but of showing that our unprecedented present is incomprehensible without Christianity.

MT: I'd like to hazard a biological metaphor. The most beautiful of life's mechanisms, the conception of a child, pregnancy, can morph into a terrifying bomb inside the mother's body when something goes wrong, when, for example, the fallopian tubes are obstructed and the fertilized egg can't reach its normal place in the uterus: it develops all the same, right where it is, causing everything to rip apart. One has the sense that, after Christ's visit, the Earth is in turn pregnant with the Revelation that you're talking about, and that it will blossom, whatever the cost.

This formulation enables me to unleash the following devastating argument [*laughter*]: as you see it, the unification of humanity is a divine or at least a superhuman process. There's no way to stop it, whether you see it as Good, because it's divine; or whether you see it as Evil, because it's "natural," like volcanic eruptions or earthquakes.

There's thus no sense in wanting the unity of mankind, because it's happening all by itself. What must be maintained is diversity, which is under threat: diversity alone is human. Your move!

RG: I agree, but can "maintaining diversity" become a concrete undertaking for the individuals that we are? In our era, it's very difficult not to think about religion only in terms of social advantages and disadvantages. This is to reduce it to something utilitarian and to make the social our true god. In spite of my interest in society, I oppose this tendency. I'm seeking to show that the world today is unthinkable without Christianity. Period. My goal in doing this is more apologetical than it is political or social.

Our world reflects an unfaithful kind of Christianity, perhaps after the fashion of the individual in the Gospels who is delivered of the demon who possesses him but who doesn't take the opportunity to give his life a positive content, and the demon seizes the occasion to move back in, accompanied by seven of his fellow demons, all of whom are even more wicked than him. This man symbolizes precisely the generations who misheard the Good News. We must take care not to end up like him. But we mustn't hold Christianity responsible for the seven extra demons who are plaguing us.

MT: In primitive societies, the mimetic crisis culminates in a phase of unbearable undifferentiation that is resolved by the violence of sacrifice. By the same token, on a global scale, whereas in Christ's day the planet was highly differentiated, today the Earth is being unified right before our eyes: doesn't that mean we're getting close to a mimetic crisis and, thus, to a global sacrifice?

RG: Perhaps, but not necessarily. In my view, the mimetic crisis that we're living through is very different from those of primitive societies: it cannot resolve itself because it cannot escalate in the way that crises that truly produced myths and rituals could. Even though it hasn't immunized us against mimetic desire and even though regressions are always possible, the Christian, modern world has raised our "escalation threshold" a great deal; our societies hardly ever experience phenomena of collective possession anymore. We're still in an in-between zone that is perhaps the definition of what it means for History to be open-ended.

MT: We're no longer in a cycle of eternal return?

RG: Eternal return ended with paganism. Which is precisely why the neo-pagans—Nietzsche, and most of all Heidegger—strive to resuscitate it. When Heidegger said to *Der Spiegel*, "Only a god can save us,"[1] he wasn't alluding to the God of the Bible but to a new Dionysus, to a total cyclical renewal. In my opinion it's an utter pipe dream, but one that could become terrifying if there were people who took it seriously.

Christianity undoes eternal return forever. It loosens the stranglehold, but very slowly. That's why the great pagan works, like tragedy, retain a certain symbolic power in our world. Our history could be described as a spiral that opens upward, toward another dimension, one that is no longer circular. That opening is our freedom and people will use it in ways that nobody can predict.

MT: To sum up, in your view we're heading toward an increasingly undifferentiated state. But you can't have it both ways:

- either we're returning to originary undifferentiation, to the crowd, to hell, to death, perhaps even to nothingness due to generalized annihilation;
- or else paradise awaits us, but, because the future remains outside our current system of representation, we don't know how to say what it will be like.

At the beginning of our conversation, you observed that a few men of good will in positions of power would suffice to "put humanity back on the right path," convince the rich to feed the poor, and so forth. The difficulty lies in reversing mimetic desire, in putting it in the service of Good rather than Evil: many people, everyone, would have to change *at the same time*, everyone would have to become good and charitable at the same time.

RG: Nothing would be easier if we wanted to do it: but we don't want to. To understand human beings, their constant paradox, their innocence, their guilt, is to understand that we are all responsible for this state of things because, unlike Christ, we're not ready to die.

MT: The biblical story of Babel leaves me bewildered: the variety of languages is presented as mankind's punishment, and the bestowing of those languages as a maneuver intended to weaken human beings, a trial inflicted by Yahweh, who is jealous of the power their unity affords them.

I prefer not to go back quite so far, and to look at the variety of cultures as an originary given, a gift of God, if you like. Couldn't the message of the one God have been that he intended to love all of his children just as they were, in all their variety?

RG: Yes, that is indeed his message. It's not his fault if we betray him. You're forcing me to keep repeating the same thing.

MT: When the Gerasenes ask Christ to leave, to let them continue functioning in their culture, maybe they aren't wrong to do so, insofar as Christ could have unleashed more serious and more violent catastrophes than their ordinary demons.

RG: But Christ does leave; Christ doesn't stay.

MT: I wanted to hear you say it: here's an instance in which Christ himself goes away. In the end he lets them remain pagan, he lets them maintain their differences.

RG: But that's because the *hour* of Christ hasn't yet sounded for the Gerasenes. That doesn't mean that they don't need the Savior. From their treatment of the possessed man emerges an image of their collective life that seems pretty sinister to me. You're idealizing them a lot. I don't think you would exchange your fate for theirs. And why do you insist on the fact that Christianity has such a leveling effect? By making scapegoats less and less effective, it fosters communication among worlds that are becoming less and less closed off from one another. But it's not Christianity that compels these worlds to become the same. It's our mimetic nature. Christianity isn't forcing us, the French, to imitate the worst that America has to offer and to remain indifferent to the best. It didn't invent the lust for conquest and domination.

MT: Of course, but, all the same, it made the best of the situation, it used those things to serve its own expansion.

RG: It's not Christianity that makes us into the rabid tourists that we are, intent on consuming the entire planet so as to boast upon our return of having traveled more than our friends. Tourism, too, is mimetic and a source of undifferentiation.

MT: So, despite everything, you're not immune to some form of nostalgia?

RG: I'm probably a lot more nostalgic than you think. I'm quite willing to admit that in my books I've spent too much time condemning sacrificial systems. Their purpose was to contain the unleashing of violence, and thus to replace the possibility of generalized violence with a lesser form of violence, the violence of sacrifices. I'm not glorifying what's happening now, the evolution of the world toward homogenization: but I'm saying that it has a meaning, I'm saying that mechanisms of the "scapegoat" type no longer function; I'm saying that our history has as many positive as negative aspects.

MT: Everything has meaning, even overpopulation, even AIDS?

RG: It certainly does. AIDS reminds us that the sexual taboos of the primitive world had a raison d'être. The same goes for the Decalogue, whose principles are sometimes presented as oppressive: they're rooted in human nature.

MT: You make uniformization out to be the price that has to be paid for a better world, a ticket to paradise. But there are people who are just coming out of uniformization, and for them it was a nightmare. The citizens of the Eastern European countries, who were all uniformly Soviet while their freedoms slumbered, are waking up as members of a particular group, as Russians, Ukrainians, and Armenians. For them, it's part of their newly-discovered freedom.

RG: I'm not making uniformization or anything else out to be the price to pay for anything whatsoever. That's where you're wrong. There is neither any transaction nor any negotiation between religion, on the one hand, and, on the other, history and society. It's your utilitarian vision of religion that makes you see things that way. Uniformization is the search for differences, it mistakes itself for difference, because it's the source of conflicts. For example, the way in which we intellectuals seek to differentiate ourselves from one another by ceaselessly inventing pseudo-differences, revolts that are even more radical than the ones that came before, leads to avant-garde fashions that are ever more sheep-like, ever more repetitive. In a hundred years, the imperative of originality at all costs has killed creativity.

I recently asked a female Croatian student at Stanford what differenti-ated her from the Serbs. "Nothing!" she replied. "But, all the same, they're Orthodox and you're Catholics!" "That has no importance whatsoever!" "But what has importance then?" "Nothing! Except precisely the fact that we're the same!" The intensity of conflicts has nothing to do with the reality of differences.

People react out of fear to the obviously global nature of contemporary phenomena and that's what pushes them to latch on to local characteristics: how can the local context have any meaning in a place like America, where the average person moves every five years?

[*A pause*] What are you suggesting? That we dress up in traditional Pro-vençal costumes and play wooden flutes? [*Laughter*]

MT: I'm suggesting that, at the very least, for example, we try to save the treasure of our languages, if only for pleasure's sake: speaking personally, my attachment to the Breton dialect is hardly of a political nature. But I like to think that I'm speaking the language of Tristan and Lancelot, that, better still than Béroul and Chrétien de Troyes, who only recounted their exploits,

I have intimate access to the way they thought. I'll take this interior voyage over a Club Med vacation any day.

RG: Brittany is something special, but where the rest of France is concerned, regionalist authenticity is historically suspect. The regional costumes that the Americans like so much are hardly more than provincial adaptations of Parisian fashions that have been forever immobilized in the Romantic era by the modern infatuation with folklore and quaintness. What relationship is there between authentic Provence and the vacation houses that are now scattered throughout the Luberon? As for languages, I fear that French has lost the battle. The world speaks English, and, even in France, English is insinuating itself at the highest level, in research institutes and scientific periodicals.

The philosophers who are critical of modernity have shown that human rights, which were invented to put an end to various forms of oppression, have created new ones: insane asylums, prisons, and so forth—look at Michel Foucault's arguments, for example. Some intellectuals defend the idea that there is something particularly perverse about the West, which, according to them, is good at talking about freedom the better to establish its hegemony. Even if this were true, it would be impossible to prove, first of all because we're lacking points of comparison: no society before ours has taken aim at sacrificial mechanisms. So, what's revealed by all of this is the tenacity of those mechanisms. If you stamp them out here, they pop up again over there. The value of Foucault's work consists in having shown this. One day, he told me that "we shouldn't invent a philosophy of the victim." I replied: "No, not a philosophy, I agree—a religion! But it already exists!"

Foucault understood the very thing that optimistic rationalism didn't foresee: new forms of "victimization" are constantly emerging from the instruments that were intended to do away with them. It's his pessimism that separates us: unlike him, I think that historical processes have meaning and that we have to accept this, or else face utter despair. Today, after the end of ideologies, the only way to embrace this meaning is to rediscover religion. Of course, even as the victimary mechanism keeps being reborn, Christianity is always there to transform and subvert it, like a leavening agent—in the humanist rationalism of the eighteenth century Enlightenment, for example. When Voltaire defended Jean Calas, the persecuted Protestant, he was being more Christian than the Catholic priests who were against him. His mistake was to have had too much faith in his own perfection, to imagine that the correctness of his position was due to his own genius. He couldn't see how much he owed to the past that stretched out behind him. I respect tradition, but I'm not justifying History.

MT: But you are. You are justifying it.

RG: I'm trying to show that there's meaning at precisely the point where the nihilistic temptation is strongest today. I'm saying: there's a Revelation, and people are free to do with it what they will. But it too will keep reemerging. It's stronger than them. And, as we have seen, it's even capable of putting mimetic phenomena to work on its behalf, since today everyone is competing to see who is the most "victimized." Revelation is dangerous. It's the spiritual equivalent of nuclear power.

What's most pathetic is the insipidly modernized brand of Christianity that bows down before everything that's most ephemeral in contemporary thought. Christians don't see that they have at their disposal an instrument that is incomparably superior to the whole mishmash of psychoanalysis and sociology that they conscientiously feed themselves. It's the old story of Esau sacrificing his inheritance for a plate of lentils.

All the modes of thought that once served to demolish Christianity are being discredited in turn by more "radical" versions of the same critique. There's no need to refute modern thought because, as each new trend one-ups its predecessors, it's liquidating itself at high speed. The students are becoming more and more skeptical, but, and above all in America, the people in power, the department chairs, the "chairpersons," as they say, are fervent believers. They're often former sixties' radicals who've made the transition to administrative jobs in academia, the media, and the church.

For a long time, Christians were protected from this insane downward spiral, and, when they finally dive in, you can recognize them by their naïve modernist faith. They're always one lap behind. They always choose the ships that the rats are in the midst of abandoning.

They're hoping to tap into the hordes of people who have deserted their churches. They don't understand that the last thing that can attract the masses is a Christian version of the demagogic laxity in which they're already immersed.

Today, it's thought that playing the social game, whether on the individual or the group level, is more indispensable than thinking . . . it's thought that there are truths that shouldn't be spoken. In America, it's become impossible to be unapologetically Christian, white, or European without running the risk of being accused of "ethnocentrism." To which I reply that the eulogists of "multiculturalism" place themselves, to the contrary, in the purest of Western traditions. The West is the only civilization ever to have directed such criticisms against itself. The capital of the Incas had a name that I believe meant "the navel of the world." The Chinese have always flattered themselves that they are the "Middle Kingdom," and they're not the only ones. All peoples have always lived very comfortably in the most extravagant ethnocentrism, with the exception of the West, ever since Montaigne's *Essays*,² and even before.

The best of eighteenth-century literature is Montesquieu's "How can one be Persian?," and the whole tradition of the philosophical tale that goes along with it, which satirizes the cultural provincialism denoted today, not without pedantry, by the word "ethnocentrism." We don't have a lot to teach Voltaire on this subject, but he, on the other hand, could teach us quite a few lessons.

Since the Renaissance, Western culture has consistently been divided against itself. First we were for the Ancients and against the Moderns; then we were against civilization and for the savages; then, during the Romantic period, we were for the exotic and against the familiar, and so on. In our era many people think that they're breaking with tradition when in reality they're repeating it, but without the elegance displayed by their ancestors.

Very impressed by its role as scapegoat, the West decries itself as the worst of all societies. Could it be that we're entering an era in which the West, with respect to the rest of the planet, will play a role a bit like the one that the Jews played with respect to Christians?

MT: I don't think it's quite that simple. The West is rich and powerful, and the rest of the planet is rather poor; you are the first to invoke material realities when it's a matter of gauging the progress of History. The Jews, for their part, have never been in power in the Christian West. And, unlike the West, they've never condemned their own culture.

But, since you bring them up, let's talk about them. Keeping in mind the terrible persecutions they have suffered, how do you explain the "success" of the Jews? Although they've given us some of the most beautiful universal values, in a sense, no people is less universalist. You can't convert them, and they're even less likely to try to convert you. The "Chosen People" also means the "Closed People." Now, even without talking about their position in the international capitalist economy, though they represent about 0.3% of the world population, they get some 30% of the Nobel Prizes in science! In spite of two or three thousand years of persecutions, refusing Christian uniformization turned out not to be such a bad thing for them.

RG: What you're calling Christian uniformization doesn't exist. Or, if it does exist, it's linked to something that already existed with the Jews. Don't forget that the Jews were accused of atheism by the peoples who surrounded them. The Jews are indeed the Chosen People. In the Epistle to the Romans, Saint Paul asserts that their election is irrevocable. History in the most concrete sense plays an essential role. You just have to read the Bible to understand that, despite its "closure," Israel had trouble weaning itself of child sacrifice and sacred prostitution, from the kind of religion that held sway in the surrounding areas, in the Middle East and all over the world. The more the politically correct ethnologists deny the existence of primitive violence, the more the victims unearthed by archaeologists contradict their blissfully neo-Rousseauist conclusions. The fundamental texts of Christianity emphasize the fact that all the Powers of this world came together to kill Christ. Acts expresses the responsibility of the entire human race when it has Peter and John cite Psalm 2, and then offer commentary on it:

> Why this uproar among the nations, this impotent muttering of the peoples? Kings on earth take up position, princes plot together against the Lord and his Anointed. This is what has come true: in this very city Herod and Pontius Pilate plotted together with the gentile nations and the peoples of Israel, against your holy servant Jesus whom you anointed.[3]

What makes this text important is the murderous nature conferred on all cultures without exception with respect to the true God. This text reaffirms the universality of the founding murders that are represented here by the Passion. Making gods by killing victims is the human gesture par excellence and, each time that they do it, human beings widen the gap between themselves and the true God a little more, they take part in his murder.

The Passion is neither more nor less "culpable" than all the other murders of the same kind "since the foundation of the world." The Jews are neither more nor less guilty than all of us. But the Passion is the first founding murder that becomes the subject of a non-mythical narrative, an objective, realistic, historical narrative, a narrative that lets the effects of mimetic desire be seen.

Instead of telling us that the victim deserved what he got and that the murderers were right to expel him—which, I repeat, is what founding myths do, since they always maintain that the scapegoats are truly responsible for all sorts of various plagues and catastrophes, in other words that they're not scapegoats but really and truly very dangerous malefactors—the Gospels shout from the rooftops that Jesus and all victims of the same type are innocent.

The Gospels thus affirm the guilt of the Jews and of the Pagans. And their only predecessors in this affirmation are the Jewish prophetic books, which often tell of the violence suffered by the prophets. That's why Jesus says that he's going to die "like the prophets before him." You need only read the story of the death of the "Suffering Servant" in Second Isaiah, or that of the sufferings of Job, or of those of Jeremy, or the adventure of Jonah, or the story of Joseph, to see that there are already vindicated scapegoats in the Old Testament.

Once one has accepted Christianity, the only means of straying from Revelation and of not seeing that it implicates all human cultures, all human beings, without exception, is to strike out at the Jews. And that's what Christians have never stopped doing ever since they parted ways with the Jews. They must thus recognize their wrongs, which are enormous. Christian anti-Semitism is not just another example of religiocentrism or ethnocentrism—it's a failure with respect to Revelation.

And it's one and the same as the utter inability of Christian readers to identify in Holy Scripture the revelation of founding victims and of the sacrificial systems that stem from them, which we still depend on because of our repudiation of religion, which plays the same role today that the anti-Jewish reading of certain essential texts played in a former age.

As for what you call the economic "success" of the Jews, it can no doubt be partially explained by the fact that the Bible, as we've said, traces a journey from the sacrificial to the non-sacrificial, that it includes a good number of texts that anticipate the Gospels. In a sense, they're two thousand years ahead of everyone else. Just look at the extent to which Jewish people in the Middle Ages had liberated themselves from magical thinking compared to Christians. That's where their intellectual superiority comes from. Their traditions have long been favorable to study and to the exercise of critical thinking.

CHAPTER 9

Democracy

MT: Democracy?

RG: I like Churchill's quote: it's "the worst form of government except all those other forms that have been tried from time to time."

MT: Democracy is not without injustices. Children from affluent families have a much better chance of becoming big businessmen, great artists, or even great thinkers, great advocates for the poor, than do those who are born poor: because their parents are cultured, because their personal fortune gives them time to reflect and create. Although my own origins are modest, I'll take the provocation a step further: alas, many poor people who have come to power, the Communist leaders, for example, or Hitler, behaved very badly, because they were bitter and wanted revenge. All in all, then, we should accept those injustices as the lesser of two evils: what a disappointing world. Do such reflections resonate at all with the man of faith that you are?

RG: That's a little bit like what I say about America: maybe it's better to vote for the Republicans, because they're already rich! [*Laughter*] I'm thinking back on my childhood in Avignon. My parents were from the old, impoverished bourgeoisie. My father was a museum curator. We lived in a fairly working-class neighborhood, and my high school friends were the sons of low-grade clerks and office workers. And most of them eventually got their baccalaureate and managed to climb a few rungs on the ladder. Among the various societies that I'm familiar with, the French Republic doesn't do such a bad job at fostering social mobility. Traditionally, America is even more open, and the possibilities for creating a business without start-up capital are much better than in France and everywhere else in Europe. But in periods of economic crisis things can become very difficult.

MT: I'd agree that in France the schools don't really teach what kind of a society we're living in. I was prepared to take all sorts of competitive exams, I knew that I could become a manager or a functionary or an employee or a worker—in short, that I could get a job with a regular salary, like my teachers—but nobody ever told me that the most normal thing to do in the society I lived in would be to start my own business; and, of course, I was told even less about how to actually go about it. It should be taught in primary school, because it's our law, it's the law of the entire world: maybe we wouldn't stumble so much in the world markets. In your texts, you often defend the democratic nature of English law: are you sure the United Kingdom is such a democratic country? There are also terribly reactionary and brutal things about it. The colonization of Ireland was no barrel of laughs. Even today the lords possess entire islands (the Hebrides), which are half the size of French departments, and at the end of the nineteenth century they kicked human beings off them, giving preference to the sheep: that's how Australia came to be populated. All the rich neighborhoods in central London belong to the same person, and the people who live there can't buy their lodgings.

RG: I grant you that. But despite everything it's the English model of democracy that's taking over the planet, via America of course, and America has reacted very strongly against the aristocratic tendencies that you're talking about. The model is so supple, so far from being "Cartesian" in the negative sense, that it allows for all sorts of transformations without losing its virtues. In France, the rediscovery, or rather the all-too-belated discovery, of Tocqueville, is a sign of this model's influence, which is gaining more and more ground on homegrown Jacobinism, not only in the public's mind but also in political and administrative circles. Since the shift is happening via first-rate French adherents, like Tocqueville himself, it's not perceived as a foreign import. The English model implies no particular economic system. What I'm saying is not a defense of "unbridled capitalism."

MT: A Jewish friend observed to me one day that in the Biblical Decalogue, it's a matter of human *duties* rather than of human *rights.*

RG: That's also Simone Weil's argument in *The Need for Roots.* And it was one of the great themes of the conservative Catholic parties from the French Revolution up until and including the Vichy regime. Vichy, of course, greatly emphasized the priority of duties as opposed to rights.

It's only since World War II and in particular over the last quarter of a century or so that everyone has rallied behind the cause of human *rights.* And it's easy to see why. It's a theme that unifies, and it's actually one and the same as the rights of potential victims, which are set up against governments, against collectivities, against majorities that could become oppressive, or even murderous, with regard to individuals and minorities. But they shouldn't become the pretext for unwarranted privileges. In the United States, the idea of quotas was accepted in order to give minorities, in general black minorities, an advantage in school. And so the system is working to the disadvantage of other minorities. But I don't want to comment on problems that are too directly political.

The theme of human rights has become a major sign of our uniqueness as far as the protection of victims is concerned. Nobody before us had ever asserted that a victim, even someone who was unanimously condemned by his or her community, by institutions with legitimate jurisdiction over him or her, could be right in the face of the unanimous verdict. This extraordinary attitude can only come from the Passion as interpreted from the vantage point of the Gospels.

MT: You don't want to talk politics, but what you're saying isn't without political consequences that are both practical and real.

RG: Yes, but they can't be defined in ideological terms. You can draw the conclusion that we should immediately open all doors, do away with all barriers, play at being progressive sorcerer's apprentices, and you risk causing serious damage. You can also think that we shouldn't let go of anything, that keeping things as they are is the lesser evil. In general, the people on the left think I'm conservative, while those on the right think I'm a revolutionary. I say what I think without taking those categories into account.

MT: It's true that it's hard to classify you on the classical political chessboard. Here's my opinion. All things being equal, and despite the "reactionary" tone of some of your remarks, I nonetheless think you're rather inclined to open the barriers and "let everything go," in order to prove that you were right. There's something of the sorcerer's apprentice in you, because you don't know where the Revelation is taking us in this world. Given that, since the end of Communism, democracy seems to be spreading over the entire planet, do you believe in the "end of history" that the American political scientist Fukuyama is declaring?

RG: I told you earlier that I believe in an open-ended history. To think what Fukuyama is saying you have to believe in "absolute spirit" as Hegel conceived it. That's not the Spirit I believe in. Nor do I share the pessimism of people who say that after the Holocaust there's no longer any future. I think that's an overly catastrophic vision of history. The Nazi genocide is no doubt the worst of them all. Christians have their share of responsibility, Jews are right to say so, but they can only say so on a religious level. On the historical level, it's quite obvious that this planet has known other genocides. The Holocaust is indeed a terrible setback for the project that I'm assigning to our world, but let's hope that it's a temporary setback that doesn't signify that history in its entirety isn't worth living. To maintain that the Holocaust put an end to history is to grant National Socialism a spiritual victory it doesn't deserve.

MT: Some also speak of the possible melancholy that could overcome us if Paradise were finally established. Wouldn't the widespread reign of love be an extremely boring state, perhaps even too boring for mankind?

RG: You keep coming back to your earthly paradise. You must be a descendent of Joachim de Flore and other medieval heretics who dreamed of a golden age under the sign of the Holy Spirit.

The idea that paradise would probably be boring is almost as traditional as the discourse on mystical ecstasy. As a general rule, the people who are swayed by one of these discourses aren't swayed by the other. This opposition will never be resolved. Debate can highlight the disagreement but can't resolve it. Let me remind you that in my eyes the fact that all societies are becoming similar and are evolving in the same direction doesn't at all mean that they're becoming peaceful. Some kinds of wars are doubtless now impossible, for very concrete reasons pertaining to logistics, tactics, and so forth. But conflicts will take other forms. It's already begun to happen: we're seeing economic war in the rich countries and civil war in the poor countries.

MT: I was thinking of something else, of individual behavior. Our democratic societies are increasingly being ravaged by certain kinds of delinquency. It seems to me that if certain kinds of glaring inequalities persisted—and the lesson that we've learned from seventy years of Communism may be, alas, that this would be the lesser evil—we wouldn't be able to stop adolescents "without a future" from preferring the excitement of the soldier's or the gangster's life to the certainty of a miserable proletarian existence. Without even mentioning the nationalist conflicts, which have something honorable about them, look at how easy it is for the drug cartels to recruit their hit men from the poorest milieus. It's said, for example, that the networks that control auto theft and organize the resale of stolen cars in France pay four or five thousand francs on the spot, in cash, to the "petty thief" who delivers a vehicle. In a single day, these kids can easily make—and spend—several times the salary they'd earn for a month of excruciating labor in a factory. It may look like I'm reducing our philosophical problem to a few column inches in the crime blotter, but you'd be the last person to blame me for examining the collective consequences of certain human traits: won't there always be people who will choose adventure—even at the cost of doing evil—even if it's a criminal adventure—to the boredom of a model existence?

RG: The answer is yes. What you're talking about is the extreme form of what I myself was saying just now—the atomization that ultimately prevails in a broken-down society. Fundamentally, the only wars are civil wars; that's why the unity of the world means universal peace, but also, in the absence of Christian renunciation, the war of all against all.

MT: At the collective level this time, as a theoretician of desire, do you think that an inevitable flaw in democracy is that it's flooded with criminal gangs? In my opinion this isn't a marginal question: for example, if it could be demonstrated that Martin Luther King and John Kennedy were assassinated on the orders of an organization—one that was linked to the "military-industrial complex," the Ku Klux Klan, or what have you—that wanted to see racial inequalities maintained in the United States, draw out the Cuban conflict, open up the possibility of war in Vietnam, and so forth, then wouldn't we have to acknowledge that all of our high-blown rhetoric about human rights is nothing but cant and that non-Western countries might have reason for suspecting that those rights were nothing but an instrument of conquest?

RG: I don't think all of that is true; but, even if it was true, I don't see how it would oblige me to think any differently. You keep trying to make me out to be a poorly-camouflaged utopian.

MT: All I'm doing is asking someone who in my opinion has indeed unveiled "things hidden," and who offers a very fruitful and very troubling reading of human phenomena, to comment on themes which, no doubt, are my own obsessions, but which some readers may also share. How do you see the future of the world from a demographic vantage point? The Vatican remains opposed to all birth control. And yet isn't it true that if there are ever fifty billion of us, we'll end up having a problem on our hands?

RG: I think we already do. The Catholic Church's position seems unrealistic, not to say insane. At first, the desire to control the evolution of the population seemed totally excellent, harmless, devoid of any potentially disastrous consequences for the humanity of mankind. Today, the same objectivist and scientific pragmatism is asking us to submit to more and more behaviors that even those who recommend them aren't very proud of, it would seem, given that they designate them only by soothing euphemisms: in America, for example, nobody is "pro-abortion," they're "pro-choice." The real message is simple: if there are too many babies, destroy them. The fact that it's the richest members of the population who are most worried about the abortion question is doubtless not without significance.

You'll tell me that it's not a question of abortion but of birth control. In theory, that's true; in practice, it's false, but pragmatism holds all the trump cards, the combined evidence of reason and mimetic desire. There are thus a lot of churches, even most of them, who, without shouting their position from the rooftops, are giving in. The attitude of the Catholic Church or let's say instead that of the Vatican, which today is very isolated at the heart of Catholicism itself, disowned in an underhanded way by a good portion of the clergy, jeered by the entire universe, the practically official scapegoat of the media and of the whole world's intelligentsia, of every Nobel Prize winner and of every Nobel Prize nominee, has something heroic about it, all the more so because that heroism is itself unsung. We're increasingly unable to acknowledge or even to recognize true dissidence when we see it.

In the end, what makes the world foam at the mouth is that, far from displaying the hypocrisy that it's always accused of, far from adopting a "political" stance, on this issue Catholicism is quite obviously sticking to the doctrine it has always upheld. It's remaining faithful to its fundamental attitude, which consists in putting a certain definition of salvation and sin above all purely worldly imperatives of whatever magnitude.

To truly define the debate, it should be situated in the widest possible historical framework, which is Biblical, because only in the Bible can we glimpse an anthropological history, a sacrificial history of humanity that begins before the History of the historians. I'm convinced that what gives our civilization its initial forward thrust in Egypt, in Greece, and above all among the Hebrews, is the renunciation of the horrible religious universe of sacred prostitution, regicide, and most of all, of course, ritual infanticide, the sacrifice of firstborns; a renunciation that didn't occur without a struggle, to judge by the exhortations of the Jewish prophets, who, across the centuries, condemn the vestiges of those practices with the most extreme vehemence.

To say that we've already relapsed to that degree is perhaps an exaggeration; but, for anyone who seriously thinks that the destiny of mankind, as opposed to rabbit breeding, isn't decided only by economic and demographic statistics, for anyone who sees the fearsome relevance of the sacrificial principle as a means of gaining anthropological insight into our world, the least one can say is that the direction in which the world is heading, unanimously and mimetically, is troubling.

You get the impression that the fatalities of the primitive world, which the light of prophetic and Gospel texts temporarily dispelled, are reemerging beneath the mask of scientific and technical imperatives. Most human societies have practiced infanticide . . .

MT: . . . and above all the murder of daughters, which later caused a lack of women, which in turn provoked wars whose purpose was to steal women from neighboring tribes!

RG: Some ethnologists no longer hesitate to see at the source of such behaviors a sort of innate science of demographic phenomena, a Malthusian wisdom similar to their own, one that the Christian world is supposed to have inconveniently forgotten. In the Bible, the patriarchs, notably through the story of Isaac, put an end to those horrors in our Judeo-Christian history. It's hard for me not to see the current evolution as a regression, as an unsettling return to that which seemed forever transcended.

MT: It's said that the decision of the Chinese government to limit births to a single child per family has, in a few years, resulted in the sacrifice (by their parents, who wanted a son) of millions of little girls. An unimaginable and secret genocide. I've also heard that "preventive abortions" (also to eliminate girls) are becoming widespread in India ever since science made it possible to determine the sex of the fetus.

RG: Here we're in an absolutely tragic situation. It is perfectly true that, on the human level, the level of rational "planning," abortion and all the measures for limiting births are as justified as can be. The modern world seems to force people to choose between either, on the one hand, heroic renunciation, chastity, sobriety, poverty, and everything that was once deemed "saintly" or, on the other, a blind descent into chaos and death. And this in an era that is increasingly unable to comprehend the positive nature of renunciation.

I already said earlier that the battle being fought by "progressive" Christians to reconcile Christianity with contemporary society seemed to me to be out of touch with what people who have been uprooted by modernity are actually feeling. This way of confusing the Catholic Church with a political party that's a step behind its constituency is a loss of religious meaning.

MT: It's true that the call for a "wholesale liberation" leaves a great deal unsaid.

The spread of pornography has, it seems, increased the cases of impotence by putting the spectators in a position of "mimetic rivalry." When you take sexual liberation far enough you come to the last taboo, which is the other's lack of desire.

RG: The more "liberated" desire seems to be, the more it generates this supreme obstacle. I think the role of institutions is to protect individuals. Marriage freed human beings from the caprices of desire and created spans of calm and security. You've just provided an admirable formulation of our era's true problem in the erotic domain, which no longer has anything to do with the things that psychiatrists and psychoanalysts, like automatons, keep mechanically repeating. With the disintegration of the nuclear family, the disappearance of father figures makes the whole Oedipus complex mumbo-jumbo into a real psychiatric dinosaur—of the vegetarian persuasion, it goes without saying.

MT: But you find Christian complexes about sexuality ridiculous?

RG: You talk as if there was still such a thing as a Christian subculture in our society. I'm afraid that it's already disappeared. You remind me of those caricaturists from the satirical newspapers who reinvent priests in cassocks because they can't do without them. That said, puritanism is like the witch hunt: when these phenomena flare up, that means they're going to disappear. Like its opposite, puritanism is nothing but a temporary manifestation, an error less disastrous than the sexual hysteria that's disorienting our world and that has nothing to do with the liberation it promises. With every instant that passes, the world we live in confirms not only Christian morality but all great religious moralities.

MT: You spoke of "tragedy" with respect to the trends in world population. So, I'm going to ask you *the* question once more. Far from carrying out divine will, aren't we instead in the process of rebuilding Babel, of defying God? If the conclusion of history was quite simply the end of the world, absolute catastrophe, the extinction of all mankind (like that of the dinosaurs in the Mesozoic period) due to a thermonuclear war or a viral epidemic or something else, the Christian promise would look pretty silly wouldn't it? And in our absence the angels could argue about whether Christ merely announced or actually *created* the mortal Fall.

RG: Why would it look silly? Why do you want to incriminate Christianity when its influence on the powers that govern us is vanishingly small? We have enough scientific knowledge and enough technical means to ward off the threats that are said to hang over the world; now all we need is to actually want to ward them off. Our little mimetic rivalries remain our priority. Unable to gain access to the true themes of our time by daring to transgress our society's true taboos, we keep beating the dead horse of sexual puritanism, keep trotting out the same old derision, with mechanical violence, in the glacial chill of nothingness; or else, to the contrary, we feign the exaltation of sham liberations, we "mimic" the old surrealist nonchalance and brandish the everlasting shreds of a culture in tatters.

Today, most intellectuals and artists are light-years away from popular sensibilities, for it's true that the apocalyptic spirit, which is integral to both Christianity and Judaism, is as alive as it's ever been. I recently read in an American sociology publication that more than sixty percent of New Yorkers believe that the end of the world is imminent. True, fervent Christians have always had this impression, even if they never hoped it would happen; there's no death wish in them. In the past—and it continues today—apocalyptic belief was the target of innumerable jibes. Yet at other moments the very same people who make a ritual out of mocking that belief write extremely learned essays on the latest ecological panics and the possible destruction of all life on our planet. We do everything possible to avoid mixing these two literary genres. Nobody explains to us what makes the practitioners of the first imbeciles and of the second scientific oracles. If we want to renew our sense of the comic, we should start making a little fun of all the scholars who, until very recently, thought our world was completely eternal and for whom, not long before Darwin, the idea that species might go extinct was inconceivable. The true return of religion isn't the one the media talks about. It's the one that does away with the barriers, which we hold to be impermeable, between religion and everything else. The more "progressive" it becomes, the more atheistic science is "apocalyptic," as much and even more so than religion, but in an entirely sinister fashion. Now that's something we should be discussing at academic conferences. That's what a truly vital and contemporary culture, if it existed, would somehow manage to delve into.

MT: Isn't the Christian paradise, which "is not of this world," a sort of Platonic "idea" that detaches people from the earth? Aren't Christians to some extent responsible for the ecological disaster that we're experiencing here below (which would provide another link between Christianity and Marxism—see the Aral Sea, the Baltic, Chernobyl . . .)?

RG: No, because human beings are the keepers of the garden. Besides, outlooks on this issue have changed a great deal. Until now, it was thought that only the capitalists ignored environmental concerns provided they could make a profit. And now we're realizing that the communists did worse things in the name of improving the proletariat's standard of living. That said, I'm quite willing to acknowledge Christianity's indirect responsibility, given that it made science and industry possible and put an end to slavery. If there were slaves, as in Aristotle's republic, there would be no pollution—they'd be given brooms. There is always a price to pay, because human beings are not what rationalist utopians and others tell us they are. In my childhood, the "progressives" criticized the Biblical God for hindering technical progress. Today, the same people are criticizing it for the opposite reason.

MT: Have you ever asked yourself what would happen if contact was established with an extraterrestrial civilization? How might that change the evolution of the world, philosophy, your thought, Christianity?

RG: You're no doubt aware that in America huge amounts of money have been and are being spent to try to detect traces of life somewhere, anywhere, in the solar system or elsewhere. They've never met with the slightest success, but they keep at it anyway. This stubbornness has something touching about it that could be likened to an anti-religious religion. It's no longer a matter of denying the existence of extraterrestrials, as in the past, but to the contrary of proving that they exist and that their existence demonstrates the falsehood of a religion centered on mankind, that is to say on the real problem. It's thought that making contact with these extraterrestrial minds would "put the finishing touches on" the refutation of Christianity.

We can draw two conclusions: the first is that the refutation of Christianity is still incomplete; the second is that making contact with extra-humans, for reasons that remain obscure, is perceived as decisive from a religious point of view. If such contact was made, it would be very exciting and no doubt very moving, but I don't see why it would bring any revelations more decisive than, say, those brought by the discovery of America in 1492. How is it that so many people possess the irrational but ineradicable certainty that an extra-human intelligence somewhere in the cosmos, merely by communicating with us, would shed light on the meaning of our existence? It can only be the need for a transcendence able to put an end to Christianity, as in Heidegger. The more things change, the more they stay the same. Flying saucers are the neo-paganism of the masses.

I would be very happy if the infinite reaches of space truly became the "New Frontier" that the Americans used to talk about. There is, however, a figure that makes one stop and think—the one the experts casually let drop at the moment when the most glorious of space probes, after having spent a few years visiting numerous planets, finally left the solar system. Courageous little probe! If its batteries don't run out, it will put us in touch with the stars. It's heading for the closest of them at an unprecedented speed. We just have to be patient, as we were while admiring the photos of Venus when Jupiter and Saturn were still on the horizon. The problem is that, this time, we'll have to wait longer: one hundred and forty thousand years.

CHAPTER 10

God, Freedom

MT: Why was it necessary for Christ to die? Was it the last guiltless sacrifice before the abandonment of sacrificial systems?

RG: Well, the other previous victims weren't guilty either. Christ dies because he refuses to submit to the law of violence, he denounces it whenever he speaks, and human beings, by refusing his Revelation, necessarily direct their violence back at him. They put the law of violent mimetic desire into action against him. They make him into one more scapegoat. That's the anthropological foundation of the Passion, and it's nothing more. If the Passion were only something human, the voice of Christ would have been smothered, or he would have become a pagan divinity like the rest, a sacralized scapegoat. His real message would never have made it to us.

His voice was heard, his disciples were reconverted, and, instead of joining his persecutors, as they were beginning to do during the Passion, they finally proclaimed the innocence of Jesus, and all of this was possible thanks only to the Resurrection and to the Paraclete, which taught them the truth. This specifically religious dimension calls for a form of religious consent that dogma says is possible only through divine grace. Christ thus died to save us, to put us in a position to take advantage of that grace. God asks of all human beings that they behave like Jesus, which is to say that they abstain from violence and proclaim the Kingdom. We never manage to gain access to the religious dimension through the meager power of reason alone, but we can see that it's rational, and that its effects are too. We see that myths become legible. We see that structural violence is on the wane, even if anarchic violence is once again on the upswing.

We observe these results and we clearly see that Jesus is not an archaic divinity, a sacralized scapegoat. What he brings to us cannot come from human beings, and therefore can come only from God. That's why dogma affirms that Christ is not only a man but the Son of God eternally begotten of the Father. Jesus is not divinized in his capacity as the scapegoat of human beings. The people who imagine that the divinity of Christ is the result of the Passion have a mythical outlook, Christianity says the opposite. Like the light, he is at once what we must see and that which makes it possible to see him.

MT: That's all very brilliant, but when you say that "Christ is eternally begotten of the Father," you either believe it or you don't: it's a matter of faith. If you don't have that faith, even if you concede that Jesus isn't an "archaic divinity," even if you consider his Revelation to be the most important message in all history, that doesn't necessarily imply that it comes from some elsewhere called God—couldn't it just come from him, from his own genius?

RG: I'm not the one who says it, the dogma does. But it's important to show that the saying corresponds to real effects in many areas, effects that have nothing to do with myth, and everything to do with their destruction. Christianity has good reasons to consider itself absolutely unique. You can believe that without being an ethnocentric simpleton. Myths are religions of victorious false accusation. The Gospel narrative refutes not only the guilt of Jesus but all lies of the same kind, for example the one that makes Oedipus out to be a parricidal, incestuous plague-spreader.

Christianity sends back to human beings the violence that they have always projected onto their divinities. That is why we accuse it of guilt-tripping us. And on this point we are right, but the Gospel narrative is even more right because to defend our victims it is obliged to condemn their persecutors, which is to say ourselves.

In Greek, as I said, the Holy Spirit is "the Defender of Victims," and Satan is "the Accuser." Gospel symbolism fits admirably with the mimetic reading.

Jean-Marie Domenach thinks that I'm trying to give a scientific demonstration of faith. I know that faith is indemonstrable, but it's not alone. There's also intelligence, and the great Christian tradition has always maintained that there is a fundamental agreement between faith and intelligence. It's that agreement that I'm seeking to define on a point of capital importance, but I base my arguments on the Gospels rather than on Saint Thomas Aquinas or on Aristotle. That's why I have the fideists, the ones who say, "I believe because it's absurd," against me, as well as the old Catholics who cite Aristotle at the drop of a hat but never the Gospels. Seeing me cite them myself, they suspect me of being a "Protestant."

If what I say is true—and I think you'll concede that we shouldn't exclude the possibility *a priori*—the thought that underpins the Gospels must stem from a reason more powerful than our own. It makes it possible to solve riddles that modern thought has never solved, first and foremost the riddle of archaic religion, which is at the same time the riddle of society's foundation. As ambitious as it may be, my project has nothing scandalous or "hubristic" about it from a Christian point of view because it makes no pretense of clearing up what Christianity calls the mysteries of faith. It aspires only to show that, from the vantage point of that faith, the false mysteries of mythology become transparent. That's what mainstream Christian tradition has always maintained but has never concretely shown, for lack of a foothold in Gospel anthropology, which it has never succeeded in deciphering. That anthropology, which Simone Weil perceived, but which she didn't have time to explore, bears on mimetic conflicts, on "scandals" and the scapegoat mechanism. It reveals that, since Cain, since "the foundation of the world," all cultures rest on the founding murder. I'm not the one who says so—the Gospels do.

Without realizing it, Christian thought has always substituted a philosophical anthropology for the Gospel anthropology. And it must be said that Plato and Saint Augustine, Aristotle and Saint Thomas, were a lot better than everything that's been done since. They were a lot better than the tailspin from existentialism to structuralism and post-structuralism. Not to mention, of course, the abject failures of Eugen Drewermann and other celebrities fashioned by the media.

We've come to the point where, from repeated brainwashings, the unfortunate Christians think not only that they're the most contemptible bastards in history—this has been the case for a long time—but also the biggest imbeciles, which until recently they still weren't quite sure about. We have to show them that they're not as stupid as they think. We have to give them back a little of the pride that they once possessed, in overly large quantities, no doubt, but that they've replaced with a dreadful inferiority complex, a terrible defeatism that has nothing to do with Christian humility. I naturally get accused of triumphalism myself. If by chance I was on the money, it wouldn't only be Christian thought that could take solace in the fact, but reason itself, whose ultimate disintegration has been officially proclaimed by our valiant champions of deconstruction.

In the realm of intelligence, what counts are results, the explanatory power offered by the Gospels once you read them from a mimetic perspective, which in my opinion is their very own perspective.

MT: You already put that idea forward earlier: the proof lies in the results, you justify your hypothesis by the fruit it bears.

RG: Christianity's power is revealed on the intellectual plane. And it must be added that there's a history. God chose a single people called the Jewish people for an entire part of Revelation, and he universalized it with Christ. From this vantage point, there's obviously a failure of Judaism, but today there's also, of course, a failure of Christianity, which is even more serious, and which is multiplied by the deaths of the Holocaust. But to say that is to condemn neither Judaism nor Christianity from a human point of view. Who are we to condemn our brothers?

MT: All the same, if you believe in God, you have good reason for wondering: is God there merely to predict catastrophes, or to ward them off? How can we conceive of an all-powerful and omniscient God who gives humans freedom . . . to go to their doom if they aren't careful?

RG: History moves forward only through a series of human failures that are always balanced out by God's renewed efforts to make us aware of who He really is.

MT: Couldn't there have been some way of avoiding those failures?

RG: To avoid them, God would have had to impose his law on us by violent means. In any event, we're in the thick of the Christian mystery, and we can only bow, say that we don't know.

MT: Even René Girard?

RG: Most certainly.

MT: In a text that I happened upon you repeat a remark made by Messori, an Italian journalist, who notes that the imperfections of the Gospels, their repetitions, their contradictions from one text to the other speak in favor of their authenticity: if they were nothing but fabricated propaganda, as Renan claimed, they would have been more carefully put together. There's surely a grain of truth in that. But, on the other hand, when you say else-where that "the writing of the New Testament cannot be entirely human," you yourself destroy your previous argument, for how can it be imagined that God made mistakes which, caused by him, would in the final analysis be deliberate.

RG: God didn't make any mistakes, but the Gospels are transcribed by human beings; and these human beings, in particular Mark, warn us themselves that they didn't understand anything at the time. They only understood *a poste-riori*. Catholicism is made up entirely of tradition. The idea of going back to a Christianity that would be the Christianity of Christ is an absurdity, because all our witnesses are men who, even though they were inspired by grace, are capable of being a little mistaken. All we have are people who slap themselves on the forehead after the fact and who say: "Ah! So that's what he meant!" One fine day they become capable of remembering things that they hadn't grasped at the time. In Christianity, access to God and to the feeling of his presence is always linked to an intellectual experience, to work on texts, to the act of establishing connections between Old and New Testaments. It seems I'm also accused of "Marcionism," that is to say the heresy that consists in eliminating the Old Testament: one couldn't be more utterly mistaken about my work.

MT: I insist: why does your thesis require the hypothesis that God exists? I'm almost inclined to think that it weakens it.

RG: Absolutely not. What I believe seems to me very luminous, but what I say is much less so. It's quite apparent to me that Revelation, even today, far from being exhausted, contains unfathomable reserves of intellectual and spiritual power, reserves that have previously been identified, but whose specific aspects we can now define as never before. I'm therefore convinced that my intellectual and spiritual adventure isn't only subjective. It's not merely a product of academic narcissism, from which I'm not exempt, I know. My personal failings probably make me less effective but they have nothing to do with the crux of the matter.

MT: I'll start over: why does Jesus have to actually be a god or the God, and not simply a man of genius who said what had to be said? What does that change?

RG: You're talking about the sum and substance of faith, the dogma of Incarnation. Christ preferred to die rather than take part in violent sacrifices. When a man lives and dies as God the Father would have lived and died if he had come down to earth, he is himself God: only one man ever did that, and that's Jesus Christ. But you shouldn't get caught up in a "genetic" vision of things, you shouldn't think: "He became God." What Christianity says is that he was sent by God. In other words, God is the one who has the initiative in Revelation. And that's what I think. God has the initiative in Revelation, but Jesus is fully human.

MT: When one hears you talk like that, hears you say that "Jesus is sent by God," one has the impression that God is a person.

RG: But God is a Person! In fact he's three Persons in a single God! That's dogma itself! The word *persona* is a Greek word that means "actor." We mustn't bemoan the fact that the word has a literary and theatrical origin, because it's a concept that is absent from philosophy and that had to be borrowed from literature, which is always stronger than philosophy where existential relationships are concerned.

MT: Couldn't it be said that "Jesus behaves like God" because *he creates God* by planting the seeds of the Revelation you're talking about?

RG: The proof that God *reveals himself* in the Gospels is that He exists apart from us, that we have yet to truly understand the logic of his death, we don't understand what makes it so that, thinking as He thinks, speaking as He speaks, and behaving as He behaves, He had no choice but to be expelled from the world. That same incomprehension ceaselessly repeats the expulsion on the textual level. There is of course a circle, and, to make us understand that it exists and that it's closed, that circle has to open up for us a little. Make of it what you will.

MT: What does it change that God exists and reveals himself—and not that Jesus invents him?

RG: What does it change? It means that the entire sacrificial, moral, and religious history of humanity before Christianity is a holy history. It means that the pagan religions were a first path toward God, and that the practice of sacrifices was a way of keeping violence to a level that God didn't desire, but that he tolerated.

I could also toss the ball back into your court: why are you seeking at all costs to leave God out of the equation when he signals his presence, why do you always want to make everything smaller, to reduce everything to human dimensions when we know that those dimensions aren't enough for us?

And yet it's not a matter of "wishful thinking," of mistaking one's desires for reality. I can't do without God for reasons that, it's true, aren't always intellectual, but that often are, and in our era that's very important, because it's in the intellectual realm that, since the eighteenth century, Christianity has been pronounced utterly defeated and completely discredited.

I'm not the one who reads myth from the vantage point of the scapegoat, the Gospels do. The Gospels are borne aloft by an intelligence that does not come from the disciples and that is clearly beyond everything that you, me, and all of us can conceive without them, a reason that is so superior to our own that after two thousand years we are discovering new aspects of it. Here we have a process that surpasses our understanding because we were unable to conceive of it ourselves; and yet we're capable of taking it in, or we soon will be. The process is therefore perfectly rational, but it stems from a higher reason than ours. In my view, we have here a new illustration of a very great traditional idea, reason and faith upholding each other. *Fides quaerens intellectum* and vice versa.

That's a Thomist way of reasoning, I think, but it's applied to a domain—anthropology—that in Saint Thomas's era didn't exist in the modern sense. And, once more, it's a question of the Light that is at once what must be seen and what makes it possible to see, *Deum de Deo, Lumen de Lumine.*

MT: All of your responses interest me, of course, and I respect them, but they're commentaries on what you as a believer hold to be true rather than responses to my agnostic questions: what about the efficaciousness of Revelation, the proclamation of the victim's innocence, the news of the earth's unification, and so forth, would change if it had been invented and expressed by a man?

RG: But it was invented by a man. Jesus's humanity must be taken just as seriously as his divinity. That's what the Incarnation is. To be Christian is to believe that the proclamation you're talking about has only one source and that he is at once God and man. Add to that the Paraclete, who also has to be there since he's the defender of victims, and you have the Trinity that everyone today gets so worked up about, as if it were the most ridiculous thing in the world.

The crucifixion shows that human beings reject God's truth and that God, not wanting to triumph by force, which wouldn't have any meaning for Him, arranges to manifest himself to human beings without violating their human freedom. To do this, he agrees to serve as our scapegoat, but without getting divinized as such, without becoming divine in the pagan sense. He shows us that God's truth cannot manifest itself without getting expelled. To truly repent the way Peter and Paul do is to understand one's personal participation in the expulsion of God. Instead of divinizing human violence projected onto the scapegoat, Christianity divinizes the one who, through death freely accepted, a death that nonetheless is not a suicide, escapes the circularity of lies and violence that generates false gods.

The proof that the true God must get expelled and that he would get expelled again if he came back to earth—as Dostoevsky's story of "the Grand

Inquisitor" suggests—is that Christ was crucified. Once more it's the circle that has to open up a little to show that it's there, and that it's closed to us.

MT: Let's take the problem from the opposite angle: if God exists, did he really *need* the Passion of the Christ, did he need this whole human story to make himself known?

RG: He needs it, I repeat, to reveal himself as he is, that is to say to respect the freedom of human beings. If this formulation is insufficient, that's because we necessarily see everything from our point of view.

MT: If God is going to take human form, why must he be born from a mother's womb, why must he have a childhood?

RG: The logic of the Incarnation requires it, provided one takes it seriously. If God has nothing to do with our violence, with "human glory," which is purchased at the cost of mimetic rivalries, and thus of violence and vengeance, he cannot reveal himself directly. Either he doesn't reveal himself at all, or else he reveals himself by undergoing violence rather than inflicting it on others. He's the opposite of Dionysus and all the gods like him, of all the thundering Jupiters. It is necessary that nothing that makes up our pitiable condition be foreign to him.

The prologue of the Gospel of John is a sort of inversion of Genesis that shows that it's not God who expels mankind, as the scene in earthly paradise tells us, but mankind who expelled God. In my opinion, that's how original sin should be defined.

> The Word was the real light that gives light to everyone; he was coming
> into the world. He was in the world that had come into being through him,
> and the world did not recognize him. He came to his own and his own
> people did not accept him.

MT: How do you understand Christ's last words: "My Father, why have you forsaken me?"

RG: It's a citation of a psalm, but it shouldn't be downplayed, it should be understood in the strongest sense. Christ experienced all of the worst things that a human being can undergo, including the experience of being forsaken by God. Man cannot criticize God for remaining in his "ivory tower." With Christ's death, God is telling us: "I've tolerated your violence in order to create truly free human beings, but you can't criticize me for it: I'm also submitting myself to that violence, I am myself undergoing the worst violence."

MT: I think I already know what you're going to say, but I'm going to ask the question anyway for the sake of clarifying our debate: are you just Christian or are you Catholic?

RG: I'm Catholic, but I think the quarrels among the various Christian churches have lost whatever meaning they once had. I'm Catholic because I think that Catholicism is in possession of the truth about dogma. It's the farthest from the extremist oscillations that began with the Reformation and that led to modern atheism. But Protestantism has great virtues that Catholics would do well to imitate. With regard to the Scriptures, it doesn't have the attitude of sacred respect that makes it so that, even today, turning to the Gospels and looking into their anthropology as I'm doing automatically arouses suspicion of heresy. It's not accepted, and even then not always, unless you can show that everything you're saying is already in Saint Augustine or Saint Thomas Aquinas. Deep down, what paralyzes Christians is fear. They know that for centuries the moderns have always oriented their thought against them, and so they're afraid of thought.

MT: All the same, the texts are considered to be an untouchable canon, aren't they?

RG: The fact that there are four Gospels instead of one, all of them a little or even pretty different from one another, contradicts the whole fundamentalist notion that the letter of scripture is infallible.

MT: Do you really believe in all the dogmas, in papal infallibility, in the Immaculate Conception of Mary, in the Resurrection of the Body, for example? Or are these just metaphors, figures of speech, and if so, why not just come right out and say so?

RG: The dogmas, to me, are not metaphors. In my work I sometimes make metaphorical readings, for example when I contrast the virginal conception to divine births as they are related in myth, which are always linked to violence. Faith is something different. I feel like I have real-life experience of the central dogmas. As for the more marginal dogmas . . . I don't always feel any particular inspiration. But it's a question of loyalty, or of trust, which is to say of faith. I have nothing to say that's peculiar to me about the resurrection of the body, but I could repeat what people say on the subject. Overall I have confidence in all the councils that have defined Christian orthodoxy for the Catholic, Orthodox, Lutheran, Anglican, and Calvinist churches.

MT: It's a bit odd, though, isn't it, to have the attitude that "I believe in the essential part, and therefore I believe in everything"?

RG: It would be odd if faith consisted in a series of independent propositions that had to be added together. It is a meaningful totality. And many things that we make a fuss about are just plain good sense, papal infallibility for example. If the Church is divine, if its doctrine cannot be modified to conform to every opinion poll, to suit structuralist and then post-structuralist fashions, in the end we have to call on someone, an ultimate authority in the human realm, and that someone can only be the pope.

Once more, it's really a matter of bearing witness. If you trust your wife overall but some minor aspect of her behavior suits you a bit less, you're not going to break up your whole relationship over that: you stay united! You can't say that you accept such and such a law of the Republic and not the others. You're a member of society, you're part of a world.

MT: That's not the same thing. We have to respect the laws of the Republic in our daily lives because we belong to a community. But believing in the resurrection of the body because it's written in the catechism is an act of blind faith.

RG: The basis of Christianity is scripture. That's why orthodoxy is very important despite its flaws and even if it doesn't know what it's doing, because at least it holds onto the text and doesn't let go. It carries that text; sometimes it's the ass from the La Fontaine fable that carries relics. The foundation of that basis is Christ. And the resurrected Christ ate fish with his disciples. The resurrection of bodies is a refusal of the undifferentiation and disintegration of the real that you were protesting against earlier. It's a doctrine that you should find particularly appealing.

MT: You must be joking: the logical relationship that you're suggesting assumes the faith that I'm questioning you about.

Are you bothered by the elements of the Gospel text that seem like the stuff of myth—for example, the annunciation to Mary, the virginal conception of Jesus, the star guiding the three wise men?

RG: I'm not bothered in the least. More generally, you've raised one of the very issues where the reading that I propose could turn out to be very useful once the misunderstandings that surround it are dissipated. I define Christian revelation as the event that wrenched the first Christians away from the power of myth, which is the power of the unanimous mimetic lie. That wrenching away remains invisible to the "wise" and the "learned" because it happens under conditions of proximity such that it is itself mistaken for a myth.

Christianity is the same drama as the fundamental myths and the major foundation stories, and in both cases the result is a religion. In the eyes of our "wise and learned," then, it has to be a myth. They don't make any distinction among religions. In reality, I'll say it again, Christianity is as different from a myth as would be the truthful account of a lynching from the account provided by the lynch mob, which is composed of "sincere" people who are honestly convinced that they acted justly. Myth is the guilt of Oedipus; the truth is the innocence of Christ.

The wise and the learned are mistaken, but the little children are not. They're not afraid of Jesus, whereas they're afraid of Dionysus, and rightly so. Some learned folk such as Nietzsche might not have ended up where they did if they'd been a little more afraid of Dionysus.

Our learned scholars cannot understand that there are two different kinds of transcendence. For them, religion is always the same opaque mass of superstitious absurdity. They don't see that Christianity sheds light on mythical religion whereas mythical religion doesn't shed light on anything at all.

It can't shed light on anything because it reconciles human beings at the expense of an unjustly mistreated victim.

As you can see, what I'm saying has nothing to do with some ethereal, mystical defense of Christianity. Either I'm right, and Christianity reveals witch trials similar to those of the fifteenth century in founding myths, or else I'm wrong, and my thesis is worth absolutely nothing. The criticisms that are leveled at it rarely get to the heart of the matter, they're ideological reactions to what is wrongly thought to be an ideology.

If the Gospel narrative tells us of a prodigious break with the vertigo of mimetic and accusatory unanimity, which generates myths, we must not be surprised if, in the face of a pressing mythical temptation, some mythical vestiges subsist on the margins, in the interstices, as well as a tendency to use the languages of myths and the great symbols of mythical thinking to say certain things.

It becomes possible to adhere to the fundamental truth of the Gospels, and to affirm the Resurrection, without getting caught up in the occasional detail that disturbs our intellectual habits, conditioned as they are by science.

Take, for example, Peter's betrayal. The phrase "before the rooster crows" or "before the rooster has crowed three times" makes it seem as though the Gospels make Jesus out to be a soothsayer in the naïve sense, a fortune teller who predicts what's going to happen. Jesus is thought to "predict" that a rooster will miraculously crow at the very instant of Peter's betrayal. Readers who aren't sufficiently attentive conclude that the crux of the text is the miracle of the rooster. In reality, it's probably just a question of marking the time of day. What Jesus is predicting is that, before the night of his arrest is over, Peter will deny him. The prophecy is elicited by the obvious arrogance of Peter, who, having been put in his place a first time for having reacted with indignation to the first announcement of the Passion, corrects his aim and is mimetically over-zealous in the other direction: he declares himself ready to die with his master if necessary. Jesus foresees the betrayal because he observes, in Peter and in the other disciples, what we, as readers of the Gospels, also observe if we read carefully, namely an inability to resist the all-powerful sway of mimetic contagion. He foretells that he will be completely abandoned once his arrest confirms that the authorities are hostile towards him. He knows what human nature is and isn't capable of.

It's easy to see what probably happened. The Gospels were written thirty or forty years after the Passion. The people who are drafting them get the important parts right, Jesus's extraordinary insight and the love that, in spite of everything, he bears his disciples. But, as the writers are themselves overcome by admiration and have a tendency to mythologize a little, they zero in on the rooster, and they make a "miracle of the rooster" out of a perspicacity that is most certainly superhuman but that is also very natural, rooted in a logic that is humanly accessible, the same one that mimetic theory tries to conceptualize.

What's remarkable is that we can now reinstate the higher rationality of the scene by making apparent what I would call a minor mythologization. To let ourselves be scandalized by the rooster is to understand nothing about Peter's betrayal, and in the end it is to fall back into—and to blow all out of proportion—the same illusion as the writers, namely the illusion that the rooster is very important. It's the same naïveté as the disciples, the same utter inability to see mimetic desire, but now it works to the text's detriment, it destroys the true message, whereas the writers poeticize that message but do not truly betray it. The Gospels provide us with all the elements of mimetic analysis that are eliminated by false modern demystifications. The latter see only the rooster, so as to make fun of it. My analysis does not contradict transcendence but it seeks signs of it that are more satisfying to modern intelligence than a miraculous rooster.

CHAPTER 11

Freud, and a Few Others

RG: What I like about Freud is a certain kind of analysis, a way of writing, and of working with texts. What I don't like is his fundamental prejudice against culture and against the family: *Civilization and Its Discontents*, "the Oedipus complex." What Freud doesn't see is that social and religious institutions have an essentially protective function. They decrease the risk of conflict. Of course, it sometimes happens that they do so in a violent way inasmuch as they limit certain forms of freedom. In truth, cultural prohibitions aren't there to prevent people from having fun, but to make vengeance impossible: to separate potential antagonists by forcing them to choose different objects, preventing mimetic rivalries.

MT: But nothing breaks those bonds and dissolves those barriers like Christianity does by liberating the individual. "You will leave your mother and father . . ." You're practically taking up the defense of archaic sacrificial structures.

RG: Those are the structures that Freud talks about. Yes, I take up their defense against the idea that they are fundamentally neurotic. They're very realistic. As I already said in *Violence and the Sacred*, Freud came very close to the mimetic system, it really bothered me when I was starting to work, it cost me a lot of time, to the extent that I could see the ambiguity of my relationship to Freud. I had a tendency to think—and a lot of people think this today—that my hypothesis was nothing but bad Freud, simplified Freud. As I kept going, I discovered the explanatory power of mimetic desire, even in specifically Freudian domains like psychopathology. The argument's elegance remains a fundamental criterion: you suddenly see that there is a single explanation for a thousand different phenomena, masochism, sadism, and so on.

MT: But can't the elegance and simplicity of the explanation also be a trap? How is it a criterion of truth? After all, maybe the world is all twisted and messy, and maybe the system's elegance is only in our minds, in our logic and language. Suppose that "simplicity" was just a "simplification"?

RG: Of course it's always possible, but when you study a complicated problem and all of a sudden a very simple hypothesis illuminates all of its facets, while less simple hypotheses flounder miserably, it's hard not to think that one has the right solution, wouldn't you agree?

If you never get your hands dirty, there's nothing more tempting than to criticize the traditional preference for the "most elegant" solution, nothing more tempting than to see it as a kind of intellectual preciosity. In reality, it's quite the contrary. When you're trying to demonstrate something, elegance means maximum efficiency at minimum cost. Concretely speaking, it's unbeatable. Those who say the opposite never grapple with real problems. Our world is succumbing to the allure of sham complexity. It establishes your reputation as a researcher, gives you a scientific air. "A mathematical model for everything—or death!" That's our motto!

But I agree that the possibly illusory nature of the most elegant demonstrations must be acknowledged. Where the human order is concerned, I think, false solutions abound, but they're often, perhaps always, due to flights of unconscious mimetic enthusiasm. The position I'm defending is, by definition, as wary as can possibly be of this danger.

MT: What do you think of the famous "death drive" introduced by Freud?

RG. It's a good example of pointless complication. In my view, the death drive exists, but it is entirely linked to mimetic rivalry. Mimetic desire makes you into the rival of your model: you fight with him over the object that he himself pointed out to you. This situation reinforces desire and increases the prestige of the obstacle as such. And the supreme obstacle, of course, is death, it's what can kill you. The death drive is the logical outcome of this mechanism. But Freud is unable to link this paradoxically narcissistic desire for a biological, inanimate state to the other phases of the process; nor even, to use his own concepts, to link it to the Oedipus complex, for example, even though he's perfectly aware of the latter's mimetic nature. He contents himself in some sense with adding an extra drive. This motley assemblage inspires awe in the credulous, but if it can be simplified, we have to simplify it.

MT: This is the question that comes to mind as I listen to you: "death drive" or "drive to murder"?

RG: [*A pause*] It's the same thing! And eroticism tends toward both. Just think about the symmetry of the processes at play. Take Romeo and Juliet, who are defined perfectly by Friar Lawrence: "These violent delights have violent ends" (*Romeo and Juliet*, II, vi, 9). It's always forgotten that Shakespeare starts by showing us the young Romeo madly in love with a woman who wants nothing to do with him. Shakespeare's plays always contain things that contradict in spectacular fashion the conventional—and stubbornly romantic—image that, in spite of everything, we have of them. The cult of the obstacle drives human beings from their human condition toward what is most against them, toward what hurts them the most, toward the non-human, toward the inert, toward the mineral, toward death . . . toward everything that goes against love, against spirit. The *skandalon* that the Gospels speak of in relation to covetousness is the obstacle that is increasingly attractive the more it pushes you away. You want it because it rejects you. This seesawing back and forth between attraction and repulsion cannot fail to be mutually destructive and destabilizing at first, before leading to utter annihilation.

Refusing God is the same thing because God is the opposite of the *skandalon*. God died for human beings. Remaining blind to God while going for the first super model who comes along—that's what human beings do.

The Surrealists

RG: If I had been in Freud's shoes when the surrealists came to see him, I would have reacted like he did. He said: "What fanatics!"

They're really just spoiled children who set fire to the curtains knowing that daddy, mommy, and the firemen will always be there to clean up after their foolishness and to admire them. You can already sense the spirit of May '68 at its most comical in their behavior: the bourgeois parents who say "Don't forget your scarf!" to their children as they go out to play revolution . . . Revolution as an article of consumption.

Marx

MT: We've already spoken a little about this, there are no doubt similarities in form if not in content between Marxist and Christian eschatology: the idea of a paradise to come.

RG: Unlike Nazism, Marxism wants of course to save victims, but it thinks that the process that makes victims is fundamentally economic. Marxism says: "Let's give up the consolations of religion, let's get down to serious business, let's talk about caloric intake and standards of living, and so on." Once the Soviet state is created, the Marxists see first of all that the wealth is drying up and then that economic equality doesn't stop the various kinds of discrimination, which are much more deeply ingrained. Then, because they're utopians, they say: "There are traitors who are keeping the system from functioning properly"; and they look for scapegoats. In other words, the principle of discrimination is stronger than economics. It's not enough to put people on the same social level because they'll always find new ways of excluding one another. In the final analysis, the economic, biological, or racial criterion that is responsible for discrimination will never be found, because it's actually spiritual. Denying the spiritual dimension of Evil is as wrong as denying the spiritual dimension of Good.

Sartre (and Virginia Woolf)

RG: What makes Sartre seem a little ridiculous today, though it's also touching and even worthy of admiration, is his desire to have a philosophical "system." Like Descartes. I myself have been accused of building a system, but it isn't true. I'm not just saying that to seem up-to-date, I'm too old for that sort of thing.

I find the analyses of the other's role in what Sartre calls "the project"—the café waiter in *Being and Nothingness*—the analyses of bad faith, and of coquetry, to be marvelous. It's all very close to mimetic desire. He even invented a metaphysical category that he calls "for the other," "for others." But, strangely, for him, desire belongs solely to the category of the "pour-soi," "for itself." He doesn't see that the subject is torn between the Self and the Other. And yet he admires Virginia Woolf, who shows this agonizing struggle in admirable fashion, notably in *The Waves*. This is another example of the superiority of the novel over philosophy. Deep down, Sartre was very comfortably petit bourgeois, a lover of tourism, and too even-keeled to become a true genius.

The Structuralists

RG: Modern structuralism is floating in a void because it doesn't have a reality principle. It's a kind of idealism of culture. You're not supposed to speak of things, but of "referents": the real is conceived in linguistic terms, instead of bringing language back down to reality, as was done back when the real was real. This way of thinking knows nothing but difference. It cannot comprehend that the same, the insistently identical, correspond to something real. From the structuralist point of view, there is no difference between a class of real objects and a class of monstrous objects, which in my opinion are a trace left by the disorder of mimetic crisis, without which the genesis of myth cannot occur. Structuralism studies sequences with real women and real jaguars, on the one hand, and, on the other, sequences with jaguar-women, and it puts them all on the same level.

Durkheim, at least, was able to say: "How curious, there are real differences in mythical thinking—human intelligence is beginning to function—but there are also false categories. Primitive thought is sometimes based on divisions that are similar to our own, and sometimes on totally meaningless categories." Structuralism does an admirable job of highlighting differences. But if you study the development of human thought, you have to come right out and admit that modern rationalism isn't the equivalent of myth, because it has done away with the jaguar-women. If there were dragons in the user's manuals of Toyotas and Nissans, it's unlikely that the Japanese auto industry would have succeeded in spreading its products all over the world.

After Darwin

MT: What do you think of the "creationists" who take the Bible literally?

RG: They're wrong, of course, but I don't want to speak ill of them because today they are the scapegoats of American culture. The media distorts everything they say and treats them like the lowest of the low.

MT: But if they're wrong, why not? You speak of scapegoats, but, as far as I know, nobody's putting the creationists to death, are they?

RG: They're ostracized from society. It's said that Americans can't resist peer pressure, and it's generally true. Just look at academia, that vast herd of sheep-like individualists: they think they're persecuted, but they're not. The creationists are. They're resisting peer pressure. I take my hat off to them.

MT: But what if they're absolutely wrong? For someone who places such emphasis on the truth, whatever the cost, I suddenly find you very indulgent.

RG: And what do you do with freedom of religion? In America, as elsewhere, fundamentalism results from the breakdown of an age-old compromise between religion and anti-religious humanism. And it's anti-religious humanism that is responsible for the breakdown. It espouses doctrines that start with abortion, that continue with genetic manipulation, and that tomorrow will undoubtedly lead to hyperefficient forms of euthanasia. In at most a few decades we'll have transformed man into a repugnant little pleasure-machine, forever liberated from pain and even from death, which is to say from everything that, paradoxically, encourages us to pursue any sort of noble human aim, and not only religious transcendence.

MT: So there's nothing worse than trying to avert real dangers by means of false beliefs?

RG: Mankind has never done anything else.

MT: That's no reason to continue.

RG: The fundamentalists often defend ideas that I deplore, but a remnant of spiritual health makes them foresee the horror of the warm and fuzzy concentration camp that our benevolent bureaucracies are preparing for us, and their revolt looks more respectable to me than our somnolence. In an era where everyone boasts of being a marginal dissident even as they display a stupefying mimetic docility, the fundamentalists are authentic dissidents. I recently refused to participate in a supposedly scientific study that treats them like guinea pigs, without the researchers ever asking themselves about the role of their own academic ideology in a phenomenon that they think they're studying objectively, with complete and utter detachment.

CHAPTER 12

A Method, a Life, a Man

MT: We've put a lot of emphasis on the unconscious nature of the mechanisms and phenomena we've been talking about. Which leads me to the following, rather paradoxical, question: in the end, does it help to reveal Revelation, to talk about it explicitly as you're doing?

RG: What do you mean by "does it help"? If religion is the truth, "it helps" more than we can imagine. If Christianity is false, what we're doing has no value whatsoever.

MT: I'll modify my question. Shakespeare doesn't speak *explicitly* about mimetic desire, he doesn't talk about it in his plays, he allows us to intuit its existence by showing us characters who are tangled in its web.

RG: He indeed does what you're saying, but at the same time he offers commentary and explanations. When I'm working on an author, it's no doubt possible that, in my enthusiasm, I sometimes exaggerate the revelatory value of what he's saying. And yet whenever I open up my Shakespeare, I'm never disappointed. I wrote a book on him in part, it's true, because of the content of his plays, which is extraordinary, but even more so, perhaps, because of the dozens of expressions that he plants in strategic places and that define the mimetic process from start to finish. In the comedies, it's of course mimetic desire that is featured, but in the tragedies, above all *Julius Caesar*, it's the scapegoat mechanism and sacrifice.

The night before his collective assassination, for example, Caesar has a bad dream: the Romans run toward him joyously to bathe their hands in his blood. Foreseeing the danger, his wife persuades Caesar not to go to the senate. All of that is already in Plutarch, whom Shakespeare follows very closely. But, at this particular moment, our author adds something all his own, and it's a second interpretation of the dream. One of the conspirators comes looking for Caesar, and, in order to entice his victim to the senate where his murders are lying in wait, he reinterprets the dream in a way that shouldn't reassure a man who is worried for his life but that flatters Caesar's gigantic ambitions. He predicts the future transfiguration of his collective murder, the transfiguration that will make him into the tutelary god of the Empire, the founding scapegoat of the political regime that will emerge after the Republic. "From you great Rome/ Shall suck reviving blood" (*Julius Caesar*, II, ii, 87–88). You have to admit that, for someone who's interested in the idea of a founding murder, that's worth taking note of! Of course, to truly appreciate it, you have to read Shakespeare in his native tongue, which is inimitable. He's not only the Corneille and Racine of English literature, but also its Montaigne, with everything that comparison implies in terms of a linguistic flavor that has since been lost. Don't even get me started on Shakespeare.

MT: Why didn't Christ write?

RG: Christ didn't write, but he is identical with his word. He is the Verb, the true *Logos*. He dies for the reasons that cause him to speak. He speaks for the reasons that cause him to die. The specifically Christian revelation is clarified only after the fact, in the Spirit's descent, which is the fruit of Christ's *sacrifice*. The germ of Christianity resides in the fact that a perfect imitator of God cannot fail to be killed by other human beings, because he lives and talks just as God would speak and live if He were himself on this earth. That man is therefore one with God, he is God. Thanks to him God is now present among us. Everything that Christ conquered by escaping the world and its violence without taking part in it, He offers to all human beings who are willing to let themselves be raised up by grace. Christ's act reestablishes the connection between God and human beings that had been damaged by original sin.

Above, I used the word *sacrifice* to mean the giving of oneself even unto death. This is not at all what sacrifice means in archaic religions. In fact, it's a complete reversal. In the past, I was too exclusively insistent on the difference between the two. I wanted to show that those who accuse Christianity of ultimately being just like human sacrifice, cannibalism, and so on, are wrong. I put too much emphasis on that difference, and not enough on the ultimate symbolic unity of sacrifice, which, if one examines all of the term's meanings, sums up humanity's entire religious history. Christians are right to use the word "sacrifice" for Christ: they grasp that unity intuitively and, in any event, those who aren't ready to understand certain things will never be convinced by logical and anthropological arguments.

MT: Well, at this religious level, it looks like I'm going to have trouble pursuing my line of questioning about writing. It still seems odd that someone who obviously wanted to leave an eternal message wouldn't chose to set it down in writing himself, once and for all, nipping any and all possible future distortions in the bud. Unless, of course, he foresaw a danger. You're familiar with the text from Plato's *Phaedrus* in which Plato (in writing!) has Socrates (who also didn't write anything) badmouth writing: "Writing, which cannot itself respond, as a master could, to the pupil's questions," and so forth. I would even add that History has taught us that the fixedness of writing can be a handicap: it also perpetuates errors, and above all it makes it possible for demagogues to alter a text's meaning while appearing to respect it word for word. The history of both Christianity and socialism are full of such misappropriations.

RG: You just answered your own question. One can't prevent all future distortions by putting down in writing a message that's simply "true," exempt from any sort of ambiguity. Writing and speech issue from our sacrificial origins and are thus fundamentally insufficient. Only the death of Christ is perfect, and all the writings that reproduce it suffer from an essential and necessary imperfection. It's this insufficiency of all transmission, of all communication, that justifies the existence of multiple written accounts, of not one but four canonical Gospels, each different from the others, whose drafters, moreover, are always emphasizing their lack of comprehension. Christianity is not a "religion of the book" the way Islam and Judaism are.

MT: Not only doesn't Christ write, but he seems mistrustful of any sort of logical demonstration, of the essay, if you will. He prefers to speak in parables, he tells stories.

RG: Yes, but the Gospels themselves say that the parables are aimed at the crowd rather than directly at the disciples. They can be characterized by the fact that they reinstate a god of violence and vengeance, who is in fact refuted by the Gospels, for the benefit of listeners who wouldn't be able to conceive of him any other way. The Christian god makes his light shine indiscriminately on the just and the unjust. In the parables, that's not how it is. Those who don't obey the rules of the Kingdom often seem to be punished by divine, transcendent violence. In reality, violent actions penalize themselves by eliciting the reprisals that they indeed deserve. Violent people punish one another, like the two wicked sisters in *King Lear*, the two enemy sisters. The punishment appears transcendent because it spares nobody, but it comes from reciprocity, from mimetic desire, which makes it so that the evil we inflict on others will sooner or later be returned to us, with interest. You don't project that violence onto God unless you fail to see the reciprocity, or unless, for strategic reasons, as in the parables, you put it in parentheses. The Gospels shouldn't be reduced to the parables. There is a lot of direct teaching.

MT: Your extreme rhetorical dexterity sometimes makes me a little uneasy. For example, let me go back to the ambiguous face that the West presents to the third world. Isn't it going a bit too far to assert, as you do, that as soon as a person claims to be a victim, they're behaving in a Western, Christian way? You'll grant me that the West has made real victims who have real reasons for complaining. Their complaints are natural, ordinary. They would have said the same things without Christian revelation. Your observation undermines the legitimacy of their complaints and more or less justifies Western aggression.

RG: Their complaints are objectively just, you're right. In the archaic world, they would have been expressed within the group or among fellow groups who are presumed to be friendly, as is the case in Aeschylus's *The Suppliants* or *The Persians*. After their defeat in the Battle of Salamis, the Persians tell themselves: "We must have brought this punishment down on ourselves, because of some past misdeed."

What's extraordinary in our world is that we say to the foreign persecutor: "You owe me something in your capacity as a persecutor." The traditional persecutor would have replied: "Alright, I'm going to persecute you some more. It's clear that I haven't persecuted you enough because you're still capable of complaining." But today the alleged persecutor recognizes the debt he bears with respect to his victims. That's what's absolutely unique, that now we address the persecutor, saying: "Acknowledge that you owe me something, because ultimately we believe the same thing, we both consider violence to be unacceptable."

MT: I'm under the impression that when the Christian West points out victims, you think that's good, but that when victims of the West point out that they're victims, you judge their complaints to be inadmissible, biased.

RG: I certainly don't want to give that impression, and I haven't said anything that truly suggests it. To the contrary, I'm saying that when victims complain, it's legitimate, but only from a Christian perspective. Don't forget that for me, contrary to what Nietzsche thinks, the Christian perspective isn't just wishful thinking: it alone is true, it's the truth.

The mere fact of a dialogue between victims and persecutors is a Christian phenomenon. In a situation where persecution is taken as far as it can go, there is no dialogue between victim and persecutor. In general, history is written by the victors. We're the only society that wants history to be written by the victims. And we don't see the unprecedented nature of the reversal. That reversal makes new historical research necessary: there aren't a lot of traces of the victims, because until now the victors have been the ones doing the talking.

MT: I'm not letting you off that easy: here we are once more, walking the blurry line between universalism and imperialism. There were peoples who were fine the way they were, who kept their little local cultures chugging

along. And then the Christians come along with their missionaries, their soldiers, and their crusades. The former obviously have every reason to tell them:
"You're bothering us!" But it's then that René Girard pops out of his box and
declares: "Ah, you see! You're complaining, thus you're already Christians!"
Don't ask me to believe that you can't complain outside of Christianity.

RG: After the Roman conquest of Gaul, Vercingetorix gets brought back to
Rome to play a part in Caesar's triumph: he was kept alive for several years
exclusively for that purpose. After the parade, he's strangled, not brought to
the senate with much pomp and circumstance to negotiate "an international
aid program for underdeveloped Gaul." Never before in history have people
spoken as we speak, nor have they even acted as we act. The sort of shrewd
people Pascal calls "half-clever" see this only as a form of imperialism that's
sneakier than in the past, but they can't explain why nobody discovered it
until now.

I grant you that the richest countries are far from doing enough, but it's
astonishing all the same to note that, only three months after the end of the
Cold War, the West was thinking of nothing but aid for Russia. That was a
real first in human history.

Given that all the objective conditions of our world are determined by
Christianity, we don't have a choice, it's quite obvious. I repeat: we're certainly not doing enough. But this "not enough" is totally meaningless outside
of Christianity, and it's hypocritical to deny it. In any event, the refusal to
tell the truth is a part of that same truth, because it's necessarily based on a
secularized version of charity: "the right hand mustn't know what the left
one is doing," and so forth. When you dissect the kind of doublespeak we use
today you expose the incessant appeals it makes to Christian theology, even
in what we're forced to hide, so as to appear doubly humble.

Seen from the other side of the Atlantic all of this is probably clearer than
it is in France because, being at the heart of the system, America doesn't have
the luxury of a second America waiting there to serve as a temporary scapegoat in time of need. And then, the Americans are less underhanded than the
French, less practiced at hiding the Christian element in their divisions.

MT: I'd like to come back to what I called your rhetorical "dexterity." It's
also a result of your immense field of reflection. You have an answer for

everything because in your view everything—and its opposite—is explicable, everything can serve as proof. Nothing flusters you. One has the impression that when faced with a fact or a work that you've happened upon, you look for a way of fitting it in, but that you never have occasion to say: "Damn, it doesn't work!"

For example, you're quite willing to show that there are many obstacles to the process triggered by Revelation, that sacrificial mechanisms are hard to kill off, and that they often even redouble their violence. Thus, when Communism falls, you see that as the proof that the Revelation is underway; but had Communism grown stronger, you could just as easily have seen that as proof that the very same Revelation was generating forms of resistance. Never for an instant would you have considered the possibility that your analysis might be wrong.

RG: If I had found facts that didn't corroborate my thesis, I would have modified the latter a long time ago.

But we should come to an agreement on the nature of the facts that interest me. I'm not talking about current events. I don't pretend to have views that correspond to my fundamental insights on everything, at the drop of a hat. All I can bring to a lot of your questions are "personal opinions" that could very well change from one moment to the next. I'm probably also sometimes mistaken about what truly is a part of my fundamental insights, and what isn't.

MT: All the same, even if you can explain the vicissitudes of history and the traps of the Antichrist, it seems to me that the vestiges of the sacrificial system and the exaggerations of the Christian attitude, on the one hand, and, on the other, the various kinds of resistance to uniformization should remain objections to your theory, rather than proofs, no?

In fact, if you want to know what I'm really thinking, I'd say that, in the face of a planetary nuclear holocaust, it would be completely meaningless to say: "Too bad, we could have had paradise!" Such an event would instead be the retrospective proof that all our rhetoric about the golden age to come was just a bunch of nonsense. It would be definitive proof that all our magnificent "progress" was in truth nothing but a Satanic trap: a march toward death (while singing, if you like)!

RG: You remind me of those people who ask for "a sign," and Jesus answers by telling them that the only sign is "the sign of Jonah," that is to say the sign of the scapegoat, the sign of the unfortunate wretch thrown to the whales by the sailors who hold him responsible for the storm. What I'm saying is that Christianity reveals its power by interpreting the world in all its ambiguity. It gives us an understanding of human cultures that is incomparably better than that offered by the social sciences. But it's neither a utopian recipe nor a skeleton key for deciphering current events.

MT: But, all the same, it's not the same thing to say that Revelation will fulfill itself in the flowering of a new golden age as to say that it will end in a destructive apocalypse, is it?

RG: If by that you mean that I have all the pugnacity of an intellectual of my generation, I willingly concede the point. And my personal flaws, as I've already suggested, make some of what I say sound harsher than I would like, and, in a general way, hinder my effectiveness.

But this world that's always teetering between a new golden age and a destructive apocalypse—you're not going to tell me that I'm the one who invented it, are you? You encounter it every morning in the newspaper and every evening on TV. You're making me out to be more unique than I am.

And you see systematic analyses where they don't exist. Once you allow yourself to see the cartoonlike Christian dimension of contemporary history, it's easy to see that it's everywhere. Except that, once more, true Christianity has never promised either a golden age or an earthly paradise. Everything I'm saying is ultimately just a watered-down version of that famous quote from Bernanos: "The modern world is full of Christian ideas gone mad."

If we try to make religion into just one more means of increasing the comfort of our little lives, well, "we have a tiger by the tail." Don't blame me for this necessarily inexact sacrificial metaphor. It's a parable as defined earlier. It's the nature of the real, which isn't going to change so as to make things any easier for us, and not religion, that scratches and bites us. Our God isn't a ferocious tiger but a sacrificed lamb. We're the ones who transform him into a tiger through our utter inability to do without sacrificial support.

Christianity is not the religion of the exit from religion, as Marcel

Gauchet thinks. I wouldn't wait around for it to set us down gently in the dainty flower beds of a consumer society that's been tended and prettified by "Christian values." If I'm right, we're only extricating ourselves from a certain kind of religion so as to enter another, one that's infinitely more demanding because it's deprived of sacrificial crutches. Our celebrated humanism will turn out to have been nothing but a brief intermission between two forms of religion.

MT: We've come back to the mystery of an all-powerful and omniscient God who leaves his creatures free . . . who acts as if he doesn't know where they're headed.

RG: If I'm giving the impression that God is playing cat-and-mouse with us, or if you prefer, tiger-and-mouse, I've explained myself poorly. To try to understand the relationship between the call that comes from God, on the one hand, and on the other, the interplay of mimetic desire and freedom, I'm going to do a little textual analysis. We're going to take one of the best-known Gospel narratives, the one about the adulterous woman who is saved from being stoned. It's a slightly mysterious text, because it's not in the oldest manuscripts of John. Many commentators think it recalls Luke's style rather than John's, and that seems pretty accurate to me. "In any event," says the Bible of Jerusalem, "nobody doubts its canonicity." Here it is:

> The scribes and Pharisees brought a woman along who had been caught committing adultery; and making her stand there in the middle they said to Jesus, "Master, this woman was caught in the very act of committing adultery, and in the Law Moses has ordered us to stone women of this kind. What have you got to say?" They asked him this as a test, looking for an accusation to use against him. But Jesus bent down and started writing on the ground with his finger. As they persisted with their question, he straightened up and said, "Let the one among you who is guiltless be the first to throw a stone at her." Then he bent down and continued writing on the ground. When they heard this they went away one by one, beginning with the eldest, until the last one had gone and Jesus was left alone with the woman, who remained in the middle. Jesus again straightened

up and said, "Woman, where are they? Has no one condemned you?" "No one, sir," she replied. "Neither do I condemn you," said Jesus. "Go away, and from this moment sin no more."

Mosaic law prescribes the stoning of those condemned to death. I of course interpret this method of execution as the ritual imitation of a founding murder, that is to say of an initial stoning which, in the distant past, reconciled the community. It's because the community was reconciled that it has made this unanimous violence into a ritual model, a model of unanimity. Everyone must throw stones. This is obviously how the mimetic hypothesis explains the existence of institutionalized stoning such as can be found codified much later in Leviticus.

Stoning was only required for adulterous wives, not for husbands. In the first century of our era, that prescription was challenged. Some found it too harsh. Jesus is faced with a terrible dilemma. He is suspected of having contempt for the Law. If he says no to the stoning, that will appear to confirm those suspicions. If he says yes, he is betraying his own teaching, which is aimed entirely against mimetic contagion, against the violent escalation of which this stoning, if it took place, would be an example, in the same way as the Passion. Jesus is repeatedly under threat of stoning in the scenes that foreshadow and prepare the way for the Passion. The revealer and denouncer of the founding murder cannot fail to intervene in favor of all victims of the process that will finally overcome him.

If the men who question Jesus didn't want to bring about the stoning, they wouldn't display the guilty party "for all to see," they wouldn't exhibit her so obligingly. They want the power of scandal that stems from adultery to radiate out onto the crowd and any passersby. They want to push the mimetic escalation that they have triggered to its fatal conclusion.

To set the stage for his intervention, to make sure it works, Jesus needs to meditate a little, to buy some time, and he writes in the dust with his finger. Everyone always wonders what he might have written. It's a silly question as far as I'm concerned. We can leave it to those who are infatuated with language and writing. There's no point in going back to the Middle Ages.

Jesus doesn't bend down because he wants to write, he writes because he's bending down. He's bending down so as not to look his challengers in the eye. If Jesus looked back at them, the crowd would feel that it was being challenged in turn, it would think that it was seeing its own defiant look and its own challenge in Jesus's eyes. The face-off would lead straight to violence, which is to say to the death of the victim whom Jesus is trying to save. Jesus avoids giving even the slightest hint of provocation.

And finally he speaks: "Let the one among you who is guiltless be the first to throw a stone at her!" Why the first stone? Because it's the key. The one who throws it has nobody to imitate. There's nothing easier than imitating an example that's already been provided. Providing that example yourself is something altogether different.

The crowd is mimetically mobilized, but there's one threshold it still has to cross, the threshold of real violence. If someone threw the first stone, there would immediately be a shower of stones.

By attracting attention to the first stone, Jesus's words reinforce the final obstacle to the stoning. He gives the best among those in the crowd the time to hear what he's saying and to examine themselves. If their self-examination is real it cannot fail to uncover the circular relationship between victim and executioner. The scandal that the woman represents in their eyes is already present in those men, and they're projecting it on her in order to rid themselves of it, which is all the easier in that she is truly guilty.

To stone a victim willingly, you have to believe that you are different from that victim, and I note that mimetic convergence is accompanied by an illusion of divergence. It's this real convergence combined with the illusion of divergence that triggers what Jesus is seeking to prevent, the scapegoat mechanism.

The crowd precedes the individual. Only he who escapes violent unanimity by detaching himself from the crowd truly becomes an individual. Not everyone is capable of such initiative. Those who are capable detach themselves first, and in doing so, prevent the stoning.

There is something authentically individual about this imitation. The proof is that the time it takes varies from individual to individual. The birth of the individual is the birth of individual temporalities. So long as they form a crowd, these men stand together, speak together, and say exactly the same thing, all together. Jesus's words dissolve the crowd. The men go away one by one, according to how long it takes each of them to understand the Revelation.

Because most people spend their lives imitating, they don't know what they're imitating. Even those who are most able to take the initiative almost never do so. It takes an exceptional situation such as an aborted stoning to show what an individual is capable of.

"The eldest" are the first to cede. Perhaps they're not as hot-blooded as their younger counterparts, perhaps the proximity of death makes them less strict with others and more strict with themselves. Anyway, it's not important. The only important distinction is the one between the first ones and all the others.

Once the eldest have left, the less old and even the youngest leave the crowd, faster and faster, as the models increase in number. Whether we're throwing stones or, to the contrary, not throwing them, *only the beginning has any value. That's where the real difference lies.*

For the first imitators of those who started, it's still possible to speak of a decision, but in a sense that grows ever weaker as the number of those who have made up their minds increases. Once it is imitated, the initial decision quickly becomes pure contagion, a social mechanism.

Alongside the individual temporalities, then, there is still a social temporality in our text, but it is now aping the individual temporalities, it's the temporality of fashions and political and intellectual fads. Time is still punctuated by mimetic mechanisms.

To be the first to leave a crowd, to be the first not to throw stones, is to run the risk of becoming a target for the stone-throwers. The reverse decision would have been easier because it went with the current of the mimetic escalation that had already started. The first stone is less mimetic than the following ones, but it is still carried along by the wave of mimetic desire that generated the crowd.

And the first ones to decide against the stoning? Should we think that at least in their case there isn't any imitation? Certainly not. It's present even in them, because it's Jesus's suggestion that leads these men to act as they do. *The decision against violence would remain impossible, Christianity tells us, without the Divine Spirit that is called the Paraclete,* which is to say, in everyday Greek, "the defense lawyer," which is exactly the role that Jesus himself plays here. And he lets it be understood that he is the first Paraclete, the first defender of victims. Above all through the Passion, which is of course the subtext here.

The mimetic theory places emphasis on the universal tendency to follow, on people's utter inability not to imitate the easiest and most popular examples, because that's what predominates in every society. But it shouldn't be concluded that it denies the existence of individual freedom. By situating true decisions in their real context, which is that of omnipresent mimetic contagion, the theory causes decisions that are not mechanical, yet that are in no way different on a formal level from those that are, to stand out in a way they do not in the work of thinkers who never stop talking about freedom and who, for this very reason, thinking that they're extolling it, devalue it completely. If you glorify decisiveness without seeing what makes it so difficult, you never get out of the emptiest sort of metaphysics.

Even the renunciation of violent mimetic desire cannot spread without being transformed into a social mechanism, into blind imitation. There is a stoning in reverse that is symmetrical to actual stoning and it, too, is violent to some extent. That's what our era's travesties clearly demonstrate.

All the people who would have thrown stones if there had been someone to throw the first one are mimetically induced not to throw any. For most of them, the real reason for nonviolence isn't stern self-examination or renunciation of violence: it's mimetic desire, as usual. There is always mimetic escalation in one direction or another. Rushing pell-mell in the direction already chosen by their models, the "mimic men" congratulate themselves on their decisive and independent frame of mind.

We mustn't deceive ourselves. Though we live in a society that no longer stones adulterous women, a lot of people haven't really changed. Violence has decreased, and it is better hidden, but it remains structurally identical to what it has always been.

Rather than an authentic exit from mimetic desire there is mimetic submission to a culture that advocates that exit. In any social venture, whatever its nature, the proportion of authentic individualism is necessarily minimal, but not nonexistent.

It must not be forgotten that the mimetic desire that spares victims is infinitely superior, objectively and morally speaking, than the mimetic desire that kills them by stoning. The game of false moral equivalencies should be left to Nietzsche and to decadent aestheticisms of all stripes.

The story of the adulterous woman helps us see that social behaviors that are identical in terms of form and even to some degree in terms of content, because they're all mimetic, can nonetheless be infinitely different. The proportion of mechanicalness and freedom they contain is infinitely variable. But this inexhaustible diversity does not prove that human behaviors are incomparable or unknowable. Everything we need to know in order to resist automatic social reflexes and runaway mimetic contagion is accessible to our understanding.

MT: Thank you. That was a marvelous demonstration, and very complete—too marvelous, and too complete, indeed, for me to harass you any more in these pages. Just one question. I thought I heard you say that goodness, too, only takes hold through mimetic desire; in other words, that many Christians are only Christian through mimetic desire, so as to be like their neighbors. It seems to me that this is a vision of mankind that's extremely undemocratic. That's not necessarily a criticism, but I'd like to know what you think. Are there people who are born to take the first step, to lead others?

RG: It's excessive to say that "goodness *only* takes hold through mimetic desire." The people who take the first step aren't necessarily the ones that society calls "leaders." Taking the first step could consist in agreeing to follow instead of leading.

MT: You said earlier that the Gospel writers were just men who at the time didn't understand at all, you said that for us, as for them, subsequent intellectual reflection was necessary to get a grip on, or perhaps to create, the meaning of events. You also spoke of Joyce's Stephen Dedalus who faced hostility from the literary critics. Do you wish your work was more widely accepted? Or would it make you apprehensive to see it understood too fast and too easily?

RG: Whatever he may say, an author is never indifferent to the way he is received. If he's poorly received, he counts on posterity, or on the Apocalypse, for vengeance. You could interpret me this way.

MT: You run the whole gamut of human phenomena—individual behaviors as well as collective myths, history and prehistory, and so on. When faced with such a mass of information, do you ever feel like you're pushing the limits of the human brain?

RG: Once again I think you're looking at the wrong end of things. My knowledge isn't as vast as it seems to you. My intuition comes first, and it leads me toward vivid examples, or burns them into my memory when I happen upon them by chance. You'll tell me that I'm selecting what works best with my hypotheses. And it's obviously true. But that doesn't mean that those hypotheses are false. The examples that are less vivid at first would often be very good once I got to the end of my analysis, but it would take us more time than we're taking now. Analyses that were too long wouldn't be suitable for a conversation like this one. They're not even suitable for scholarly publications, to judge by the lack of understanding that often surrounds my work, even—and perhaps especially—among "specialists."

I'm probably partly responsible for this situation. I'm under the impression that I've never been able to lay out my insight in the most logical, most didactic, and most comprehensible order.

MT: But is there such an order? I'd have a tendency to say that you'd be hard pressed to lay out a set of ideas like yours, with so many transversal connections, in linear fashion without doubling back and repeating yourself here and there, and so forth. The global image I have of your theory isn't a line but rather an inextricable ball of twine, similar to the network of neurons in our brains. The latter is sometimes even compared to a hologram: when a wound damages a lobe, the neighboring zones learn to perform the functions that disappeared with it: *because the whole is in each of its parts.* That's why I fear, as I was saying earlier, that solutions that are too elegant and too unique are nothing but traps laid for our vanity by Logic, which I would characterize as the "Satan" or the "Antichrist" of the mind.

RG: Your metaphors are excellent, but in spite of everything I haven't given up on finding a better order. The mimetic hypothesis makes me think not so much of a very tangled ball of twine but rather of a road map that has been folded over on itself so many times that it's just a little rectangle. To use it, you have to unfold it, and then fold it up again. Clumsy people like me can never find the original folds, and the map soon tears. It's those tears that make it possible for skeptics to think that the map I carry around in my head isn't all in one piece, that it's just a bunch of fragments that have been assembled and stuck together in an artificial manner to make up the "Girardian system," as they call it, which is good for amusing the peanut gallery for a little while, before being placed on the scrap heap, next to Postman Cheval's "Ideal Palace."

If I could do just one thing in the time I have left, I would like to learn to unfold and refold my road map in such a way as not to tear it. If I managed to do this, I could then write an apology for Christianity that was accessible to so-called uncultivated people, to those who probably aren't wrong not to have followed any of what's been happening over the last thirty years in the social sciences and philosophy.

MT: While going through the transcripts of our many conversations (which have taken place over ten years), in the course of which I've often repeated the same questions, I sometimes happen upon an illuminating answer, an absolutely dazzling summary—I tell myself that maybe you yourself have forgotten them.

RG: I too sometimes have the feeling of finding something only to forget about it later.

MT: What we're saying now interests me because we have to make do with our bodies, with our human language, and because, a bit earlier, what you were saying about creation being possible "only from within tradition" left me wanting more somehow. We haven't said anything about the *new* properly speaking. It's been shown that the neurons that are activated when new ideas emerge are the same as those responsible for triggering dreams.

RG: If that's true, it's incredible!

MT: The means of understanding the sensation we're talking about is precisely to observe that in both cases we're struggling with the same phenomenon of immediate amnesia. An idea occurs to us, and, if we don't write it down, it disappears like a dream when you wake up.

RG: Exactly! I go to have a coffee, and I tell myself: "I'll write that down when I get back." And it's already too late.

Lately, I seem to have made some progress in formulating some of my ideas. Everything came to me at once in 1959. I felt that there was a sort of mass that I've penetrated into little by little. Everything was there at the beginning, all together. That's why I don't have any doubts. There's no "Girardian system." I'm teasing out a single, extremely dense insight.

MT: You've already told how after a very moderately Christian youth, you came to your current ideas, first via Proust. Personally, I suspect you of concealing an event that you've never spoke about, a mystical awakening, a veritable encounter with God, a "Road-to-Damascus" experience.

RG: To say that my youth was Christian, even moderately so, would be an exaggeration. My mother, of course, was an excellent Catholic who was at once a firm believer and very open-minded. When I tell that to devotees of psychoanalysis, they give a knowing nod. It reassures them enormously. But there are others who aren't content with a "return to the womb." Certain ladies who prod my Oedipus complex find it "rather tough, even very much so. . . ."[1] I've already been the target of three or four articles on the subject.[2] I'm extremely honored, of course.

I'm not concealing my biography, but I don't want to fall victim to the narcissism to which we're all inclined. You're right, of course, about there being a personal experience behind what I say. It began thirty-five years ago. In autumn 1958, I was working on my book about the novel, on the twelfth and last chapter that's entitled "Conclusion." I was thinking about the analogies between religious experience and the experience of a novelist who discovers that he's been consistently lying, lying for the benefit of his Ego, which in fact is made up of nothing but a thousand lies that have accumulated over a long period, sometimes built up over an entire lifetime.

I ended up understanding that I was going through an experience of the kind that I was describing. The religious symbolism was present in the novelists in embryonic form, but in my case it started to work all by itself and caught fire spontaneously. I could no longer have any illusions about what was happening to me, and I was thrown for a loop, because I was proud of being a skeptic. It was very hard for me to imagine myself going to church, praying, and so on. I was all puffed up, full of what the old catechisms used to call "human respect."

Intellectually I was converted, but I remained incapable of making my life agree with what I thought. For a period of a few months, faith was for me a blissful delicacy that heightened my other pleasures, one more treat in a life that, while it was far from being criminal, was, as the English language puts it so well, pure *self-indulgence.*

Curiously, my conversion had made me sensitive to music, and I was listening to a lot of it. What little musical knowledge I have, about opera in particular, dates from that period. Oddly enough, *The Marriage of Figaro* is, for me, the most mystical of all music. That, and Gregorian chant. I also started to like a lot of "modern" music that I'd never had much appreciation for in the past: Mahler, Stravinsky, the contemporary Russian composers.

During the winter of 1959 I was already teaching at Johns Hopkins, but I was giving a class at Bryn Mawr College, where I had spent four years, and I made the roundtrip from Baltimore to Philadelphia every week in the squeaky, clattering old railway cars of the Pennsylvania Railroad. As far as the sights were concerned, I usually just looked out at the scrap iron and the vacant lots in that old industrial region, but my mental state transfigured everything, and, on the way back, the slightest ray from the setting sun produced veritable ecstasies in me. It was in that train one morning that I discovered, right in the middle of my forehead, a little pimple that refused to heal, one of those minor skin cancers that aren't really that dangerous at all; but the doctor I went to see forgot to mention this little detail, as a result, I believe, of the extreme anxiety that seized him when, after having sized me up and listened to me for a few seconds, it hit him that I might at any moment set out across the Atlantic again without having settled the bill. Fortunately, I had medical insurance, and everything that had to be done to rid me of my little pimple forever was duly done.

MT: A *tilaka*, like the Hindus make on their foreheads before going into the temple.

RG: A religious sign. And then, a short time later, some somewhat abnormal symptoms appeared at the very spot where the tiny operation had been performed. My doctor's peace of mind was slightly disturbed by this, much less, it must be said, than the first time, while I, to the contrary, was much more upset. It was clear to me that my cancer was moving on to a new stage, and that this time it could only be fatal.

My dermatologist was severe, and, ever since that period, he stands in my eyes for everything that's intimidating and even fatal about the American medical system, which may well be the best in the world, but which is also remorseless, not only from a financial point of view but also because of its extreme reluctance to reassure the clientele, so as to avoid nourishing false hopes. That doctor reminds me a bit of those highway robbers who rapidly empty your pockets while constantly making death threats. You shouldn't even think about putting up the slightest resistance. And a few moments later, you find yourself lying on the pavement, completely healed.

In my case, the anguish lasted a little longer. It began in the week of Shrovetide. Before the liturgical reforms of the last council, the Sunday of Shrovetide inaugurated a period of two weeks devoted to preparing for the forty days of Lent, during which the faithful, in imitation of Jesus and the forty days he spent fasting in the desert, are supposed to do penance *in cinere et cilicio*, "in ashes and sackcloth."

I prepared for that Lent as never before, I assure you, and Lent itself was excellent, too, because my worries increased to the point of keeping me awake at night, until the day when they were banished as suddenly as they had begun by a last visit to my medical oracle. Having performed all of the necessary tests, the good fellow declared me healed, exactly on Ash Wednesday, which is to say the day in holy week that comes before the Passion properly speaking and Easter Sunday, which is the official conclusion of all penance.

I've never known a holiday to compare to that day of deliverance. I thought I was dead, and, all at once, I was resurrected. And what was most amazing for me about the whole thing was that my intellectual and spiritual conviction, my true conversion, had occurred before my great Lenten scare. If it had occurred afterwards, I would never have truly believed. My natural skepticism would have convinced me that my faith was a result of the scare I had received. As for the scare, it could not be due only to faith. My dark night of the soul lasted exactly as long as the period prescribed by the Church for the penance of sinners, with three days—the most important of all—mercifully subtracted, no doubt so that I could calmly and quietly reconcile myself with the Church before the Easter holiday.

God had called me to order with a jot of humor that was really just what my mediocre case deserved. In the days that followed Easter, which the liturgy reserves for the baptism of catechumens, I had my two sons baptized, and I arranged for a Catholic wedding ceremony. I'm convinced that God

sends human beings a lot of signs that have no objective existence whatsoever for the wise and the learned. The ones those signs don't concern regard
them as imaginary, but those for whom they are intended can't be mistaken,
because they're living the experience from within. I understood at once that,
if I escaped it, the memory of the ordeal would sustain me for the rest of my
days, and that's exactly what happened.

From the beginning, my Christianity was bathed in an atmosphere of
liturgical tradition. There are some conventionally anti-Christian people
who want nothing but the best for me and who try at all costs, so as to defend
my reputation in intellectual circles, to make me out to be a dyed-in-the-wool
heretic, a ferocious enemy of "historical Christianity," ready to plant bombs
in all the baptismal fonts.

By saying that the Church remained sacrificial for a long time, did I
really deliver a ritual kick after the example of all the asses who are savagely
bent on hounding our Holy Mother at present? It must be admitted that I
probably displayed some mimetic demagogy in the way I expressed myself.
I would have done better to situate my remarks in the context of our entire
religious history. But I didn't want to repeat the error of the Pharisees that
I was talking about earlier, the ones who say: "If we had lived in the days
of our fathers, we wouldn't have taken part alongside them in the founding
murder." The last thing I want to do is to condemn the faithfulness, obedience, patience, and modesty of ordinary Christians or the virtues of the
generations that came before us. We're terribly lacking in those virtues. I'm
too much a man of my era to possess them myself, but I revere them. Indeed,
nothing seems more conformist or more servile to me these days than the
hackneyed mythology of "revolt."

Remnants of avant-gardist jargon are sprinkled through my books,
but my true Christian readers weren't led astray: Father Schwager, Father
Lohfink, von Balthazar in his late period, Father Corbin, Father Alison, and
many others.

MT: A last question. You're the only person or at least one of the only people
to say the things you say, and you also entitled one of your first books *Things
Hidden since the Foundation of the World*. Are you a prophet?

RG: Absolutely not. I'm just a sort of exegete. All prophecy stops with Gospel

Revelation. Jesus's phrase, "I will reveal things hidden since the foundation of the world," is in the future tense because it's a citation from the Old Testament that he applies to Christian Revelation.

One day, after the publication of the book that bears this fearsome title, some Italian friends showed me an article from the *Corriere della Sera* in which Madame Françoise Giroud explained to the Milanese that in Paris there was a new megalomaniac on the loose who was even more hilarious than the rest of his tribe: he claimed to reveal, all by himself—hold on to your hats—"things hidden since the foundation of the world."

Every day I see people who think I made the title up on my own, and they judge me just about as Madame Giroud did. Of the first articles written about my religious ideas, a good half, I think, were of this type, though they were usually less amusing than the article by Madame Giroud, whose prose really isn't half bad, especially in Italian.

MT: But why did René Girard come along now? Why not in the year 1000, or in the year 1500?

RG: Now you're going overboard. Three quarters of what I say is in Saint Augustine.

MT: Sometimes I tell myself that, to the contrary, all you're doing is sticking as closely as possible to the project and commentaries of the apostles. For example, a little bit earlier,[3] you cited the prophet Joel, and I've noticed since that it's merely a citation from Peter at the beginning of Acts. But I think you're even closer to Paul—with a more modern vocabulary and the knowledge of what's happened over the last two thousand years.

RG: The citation from Joel is behind all the texts we're talking about, which always associate it with the Holy Spirit. Here it is, in the New Jerusalem Bible version:

> After this I shall pour out my spirit on all humanity. Your sons and daughters shall prophesy, your old people shall dream dreams, and your young people see visions. Even on the slaves, men and women, shall I pour out my spirit in those days.

What I bring to the table, I think, is a reversal of the conclusions of the comparativist movement, which was sparked by the huge amounts of anthropological research conducted in the nineteenth and early twentieth centuries. It was discovered at that time that violence, which is always collective and always resembles the violence of the Passion, is already there, everywhere, at the heart of primitive religion. This idea is correct, in my view it may even be the essential discovery of modern ethnology, which, since then, hasn't discovered much of anything.

Ethnologists jumped on this information, which they saw as irrefutable proof that Christianity is just another religion. As for the Christians, they sought to parry the blow by showing that Christianity is original after all, original in the romantic and modern sense, "aesthetically new." They didn't understand that, instead of fleeing the parallel between Christian and other religions where violence was concerned, they should have thought about it and seen that Christianity interprets that violence in a way that's completely different from primitive religion. Its originality consists in going back to the origin and unveiling it.

Paradoxically, the only one to understand this a little was Nietzsche, him again, Nietzsche in his last days of lucidity, with essential things to say about religion, things that Heidegger never wanted to hear. Let's let him speak:

> Dionysus versus the "Crucified": there you have the antithesis. It is not a difference in regard to their martyrdom—it is a difference in the meaning of it.
>
> Life itself, its eternal fruitfulness and recurrence, creates torment, destruction, the will to annihilation.
>
> In the other case, suffering—the "Crucified as the innocent one"—counts as an objection to this life, as a formula for its condemnation.[4]

It can be said without paradox, or almost, that this text is the greatest theological text of the nineteenth century. It is mistaken only about the innocence of Jesus, which isn't an argument against life, a mere "calumny" of other religions—the expression is found in a nearby text—but the naked truth: in other words, it's the lie of all essentially mythical religions that the Gospel Passion unveils by turning it inside-out like a glove. The Gospels denounce the idea that not only the victims of Dionysus but also Oedipus and all the other mythical heroes are guilty of the most varied plagues and calamities, which their expulsion "heals"; it denounces the violence of religions founded on arbitrary victims. And it's that unveiling that has been shaking the foundations of our society ever since.

Nietzsche's only error, a properly *Luciferian* error (in the sense of "bringer of light"), was to have chosen violence against the innocent truth of the victim, a truth that Nietzsche himself was the only one to glimpse, in contrast with the blind positivism of all the atheist ethnologists and the Christians themselves. To understand that the twentieth century and its genocides, far from killing Christianity, make its truth all the more dazzling, you just have to read Nietzsche from the proper angle and to situate all the disasters caused by our Dionysian and sacrificial choices along the axis of his writings, the first of those disasters being the madness that was getting ready to swoop down on the thinker himself—a madness every bit as significant as the political and historical insanity that followed.

Notes

Chapter 1. A First Overview: Here and Now

1. *The Will to Power*, trans. Walter Kaufmann and R. J. Hollingdale (New York: Columbia University Press, 1983), 142.

2. "... the inner truth and greatness of this movement." Martin Heidegger, *An Introduction to Metaphysics*, trans. Ralph Mannheim (New Haven: Yale University Press, 1959), 199.

Chapter 2. Mimetic Desire: Shakespeare rather than Plato

1. James Joyce, *Ulysses*, ed. Jeri Johnson (Oxford: Oxford University Press, 1993), 205.

Chapter 4. The Bible

1. *The Republic*, II, 378. See *Plato's Republic*, trans. G.M.A. Grube (Indianapolis: Hackett Publishing, 1974), 48.

Chapter 7. Science

1. Francis Fukuyama, *The End of History and the Last Man* (New York: Free Press, 1992). Actually, Fukuyama borrows the anecdote from Andrey Nuikin's essay, "The Bee and the Communist Ideal," collected in a book edited by Yuri Afanaseyev, *Inogo ne dano* (Moscow: Progress, 1989), 510.

Chapter 8. The One and the Many

1. *Der Spiegel*, May 31, 1976, 193–219.

2. See, in particular, "On Cannibals," *Essays*, I, 31 (1580).

3. Acts 4:25–27.

Chapter 12. A Method, a Life, a Man

1. Translator's Note: "*Duriuscule, pour ne pas dire dur.* . . ." The line is from Molière's *Imaginary Invalid*, in which Doctor Diafoirus and his son, Thomas, subject Argan, the imaginary invalid of the title, to a comprehensive (and absurd) physical examination.

2. Among others, Sarah Kofman in *The Enigma of Women: Women in Freud's Writings* (Ithaca: Cornell University Press, 1985), 59–63; and Toril Moi, "The Missing Mother: The Oedipal Rivalries of René Girard," in *Diacritics*, Summer 92, 21–31.

3. At the beginning of chapter 8.

4. *The Will to Power*, trans. Walter Kaufmann and R. J. Hollingdale, 542–543. René Girard's italics.

Index